Guide to
Adirondack Trails:

SOUTHERN REGION

First Edition
The Forest Preserve Series, Volume VII

By Linda Laing
Series Editor, Neal S. Burdick

The Adirondack Mountain Club, Inc.

Copyright© 1988 by
The Adirondack Mountain Club, Inc.

Design by Mary Parliman; also Lange, Collyer & Associates, Inc.
Photos on pp. 32, 44, 72, 98, 115, 116, 134, 148, 152, 160 and 164 by the author.
Photos on pp. iv and 144 by Ken Coulter. Photo processing by Mark Habetler.

Library of Congress Cataloging in Publication Data

Laing, Linda, 1939—
    Guide to Adirondack trails: southern region/by Linda Laing—1ˢᵗ ed.

    p.   cm.—(The Forest preserve series; v. 7)
    Includes index.
    ISBN 0-935272-42-9
    1. Hiking—New York (State)—Adirondack Mountains—Guide-books.
2. Trails—New York (State)—Adirondack Mountains—Guide-books.
3. Outdoor recreation—New York (State)—Adirondack Mountains—
Guide-books. 4. Adirondack Park (N.Y.)—Guide-books. I. Title.
II. Series.
GV199.42.N652A3442 1988   88-879
917.47'53—dc 19   CIP

PRINTED IN THE
UNITED STATES OF AMERICA

DEDICATION

To the unknown and unsung heroines who helped settle the Adirondack wilderness—forgotten women who worked alongside their men to create warm homes, often in grinding poverty; who bore their children, nursed the ill and injured, farmed, cooked, loved and danced, lived and died in this beautiful but unforgiving land—to you, I dedicate this book.

LINDA LAING

West Branch Sacandaga

PREFACE

This trail guide was a labor of love, accomplished with enormous amounts of assistance from my family and friends. For two years much of my free time, and that of numerous friends, was devoted to exploring the many, many trails and paths in the southern Adirondacks—an area I grew to respect and cherish. But the forest often exasperated, exhausted, and played tricks on me ("NOW where's that trail?")—and then would reveal extraordinary scenes in secret places seldom visited by man. I shared moments of joyful solitude with beaver, snakes, birds, and dragonflies, and gloried in the rich colors of wildflowers and blue-green lakes.

Many trails in the southern section were originally logging roads, or roads that once led to long-abandoned settlements. Many are also so overgrown now that they are impossible for the average hiker to find. Snowmobile trails have been cut through much of the area designated as Wild Forest, but many of these in recent years have been abandoned. Even those that are still used often lead across the frozen surfaces of lakes and swamps, making them most unsuitable, if not impossible, for the summer hiker.

I have not included marked snowmobile trails overgrown and unsuitable for the average hiker, or those that go to the edge of a swamp with no other interesting features enroute.

Trails in the southern Adirondacks, especially in the central and western sections, are generally moderately inclined or flat, unlike those in the mountainous terrain farther north and east. For that reason most of the trails, other than the mountain ones, are quite suitable for experienced cross-country skiers. Most, too, except those in the Silver Lake Wilderness Area, must occasionally be shared with snowmobiles.

There are some superb small mountains with outstanding views in the southern Adirondacks, and all of the best are described in this guide. Several do not have marked trails but do have bare summits so attractive and easy to reach that I have included them as bushwhacks, giving details but not specific compass directions. They should be explored with care and only by those who have map-and-compass experience.

Many thanks to my friends who shared not only their time but also their laughter, insect repellent, candy bars and water. They soon learned to double check my lefts and rights and found that if they insisted on leading they'd have to test the log bridges and go first through tall grasses and swamps. I appreciated that.

My very special thanks to Emmi Wilson, whose devotion to this project was beyond the call of friendship; to Jean Dionne, who volunteered for every mountain trek; and most especially, to Kenneth Coulter, for his sage advice and loving support.

Others who accompanied me at times were my daughter Marla Fugazzi, and Winnie Balz, Joan Berhaupt, Bob Briggs, Warren Burton, John Fugazzi, Marsha Hanson, Margie Marshall, Jennifer Perler, Diane Prevost, Gerhard, Evelyn and David Salinger, Jim Spring, Marvin Weaver, Eva Wilson, and—Sunny Bear. Always there was Inanna.

My gratitude also to the members of the Publications Committee of the Adirondack Mountain Club for their dedication and courage in initiating the Forest Preserve Series of Guides to Adirondack Trails.

LINDA LAING
Clifton Park, NY
November, 1987

CONTENTS

INTRODUCTION

THE ADIRONDACK MOUNTAIN CLUB
FOREST PRESERVE SERIES

The Forest Preserve Series of Guides to Adirondack Trails is the only series to cover all hiking opportunities on the more than two million acres of public Forest Preserve land located within the Adirondack Park. The Adirondack Mountain Club (ADK) published the first guidebook in this series over fifty years ago with the idea that hiking guides would eventually cover all Forest Preserve land; it is appropriate that the completion of this series coincide with the decade-long centennial celebration of the enactment of the Forest Preserve legislation. Each guide in this series, listed below, has been written or revised within the last few years, with the most recent (or projected) date of publication provided in parentheses:

Vol. I: *Guide to Adirondack Trails: High Peaks Region* (1985)
Vol. II: *Guide to Adirondack Trails: Northern Region* (1986)
Vol. III: *Guide to Adirondack Trails: Central Region* (1986)
Vol. IV: *Guide to Adirondack Trails: Northville-Placid Trail* (1986)
Vol. V: *Guide to Adirondack Trails: West Central Region* (1987)
Vol. VI: *Guide to Adirondack Trails: Eastern Region* (1987)
Vol. VII: *Guide to Adirondack Trails: Southern Region* (1988)
Vol. VIII: *Guide to Catskill Trails* (1989)

The public lands that constitute the Adirondack Forest Preserve are unique among all other wild public lands in the United States because they enjoy constitutional protection against sale or development. The story of this protection begins with the earliest history of the Adirondacks as recounted below, and it continues today as groups such as the Adirondack Mountain Club strive to guard this constitutional protection. The protection of many of the scenic and aesthetic resources of the Forest Preserve also rests with the individual hiker who has the responsibility not to degrade these resources in any way while enjoying their wonders. The Forest Preserve Series of trail guides seeks not only to show hikers where to hike but also to interpret the area's natural and social history and offer guidelines so that users can minimize their impact on the land.

The Adirondacks

The Adirondack region of northern New York is unique in many ways. It contains the only mountains in the eastern U.S. that are not geologically Appalachian. In the late 1800s it was the first forested area in the nation to benefit from enlightened conservation measures. At roughly the same time it was also the most prestigious resort area in the country. In the twentieth century, the Adirondacks became the only place in the Western Hemisphere to host two Winter Olympiads. In the 1970s the region was the first of significant size in the nation to experience comprehensive land use controls. The Adirondack Forest Preserve (see below) is part of the only wilderness preserve in the nation whose fate lies in the hands of the voters of the entire state in which it is located.

Geologically, the Adirondacks are part of the Canadian Shield, a vast terrane of ancient Precambrian igneous and metamorphic rock that underlies about half of Canada and constitutes the nucleus of the North American continent. In the U.S. the Shield bedrock mostly lies concealed under younger Paleozoic sedimentary rock strata, but it is well exposed in a few regions, among them the Adirondacks. The Adirondacks are visibly connected across the Thousand Islands to the Grenville Province of the eastern side of the Shield, which is around one billion years old. Upward doming of the Adirondack mass in the past few million years—a process that is still going on—is responsible

for the erosional stripping of the younger rock cover and exposure of
the ancient bedrock. The rocks here are mainly gneisses of a wide
range of composition. One of the more interesting and geologically
puzzling rocks is the enormous anorthosite mass that makes up nearly
all of the High Peaks region. A nearly monomineralic rock composed
of plagioclase feldspar, this peculiar rock was apparently formed at
depths of up to fifteen miles below the surface. It is nearly identical
to some of the rocks brought back from the moon.

The present Adirondack landscape is geologically young, a prod-
uct of erosion initiated by the ongoing doming. The stream-carved
topography has been extensively modified by the sculpturing of
glaciers which, on at least four widely separated occasions during the
Ice Age, completely covered the mountains.

Ecologically, the Adirondacks are part of a vegetation transition
zone, with the northern, largely coniferous boreal forest (from the
Greek God Boreas, owner of the north wind, whose name can be
found on a mountain peak and series of ponds in the High Peaks
region) and the southern deciduous forest, exemplified by beech/ma-
ple stands, intermingling to present a pleasing array of forest tree
species. Different vegetation zones are also encountered as one
ascends the higher mountains in the Adirondacks; the tops of the
highest peaks are truly arctic, with mosses and lichens that are
common hundreds of miles to the north.

A rugged and heavily forested region, the Adirondacks were
generally not hospitable to native Americans, who used the region
principally for hunting and occasionally for fighting. Remnants of
ancient campgrounds have been found in some locations. The native
legacy survives principally in such place names as Indian Carry on
the Raquette River-Saranac Lakes canoe route and the Oswegatchie
River in the northwest Adirondacks.

The first white man to see the Adirondacks was probably the
French explorer Jacques Cartier, who on his first trip up the St.

Lawrence River in 1535 stood on top of Mont Royal (now within the city of Montreal) and discerned high ground to the south. Closer looks were had by Samuel de Champlain and Henry Hudson, who came from the north and south, respectively, by coincidence within a few weeks of each other in 1609.

For the next two centuries the Champlain Valley to the east of the Adirondacks was a battleground. Iroquois, Algonquin, French, British and eventually American fighters struggled for control over the valley and with it supremacy over the continent. Settlers slowly filled the St. Lawrence Valley to the north, the Mohawk Valley to the south, and somewhat later the Black River Valley to the west. Meanwhile the vast, rolling forests of the interior slumbered in virtual anonymity, disturbed only by an occasional hunter, timber cruiser or wanderer.

With the coming of the 19th century, people discovered the Adirondacks. Virtually unknown as late as the 1830s (the source of the Nile River was located before the source of the Hudson), by 1850 the Adirondacks made New York the leading timber-producing state in the nation. This distinction did not last long, though, as the supply of timber was quickly depleted. Meanwhile, mineral resources, particularly iron, were being exploited.

After the Civil War, people began to look toward the Adirondacks for recreation as well as for financial gain. An economic boom, increasing acceptability of leisure time, and the publication of a single book, *"Adventures in the Wilderness"* by the Rev. William H. H. Murray in 1869, combined to create a veritable flood of vacationers descending upon the Adirondacks. To serve them, a new industry, characterized by grand hotels and rustic guides, sprang up. Simultaneously, thanks to the pioneering work of Dr. Edward Livingston Trudeau, the Adirondacks, particularly the Saranac Lake area, became known far and wide as a mecca for tubercular patients.

In the decades following the Civil War the idea of conservation began to take on some legitimacy, thanks in large part to the book *Man and Nature* written by George Perkins Marsh in 1864. In this remarkably influential book, which noted historian Lewis Mumford once called "the fountainhead of the American conservation movement," Marsh called for the implementaion of such practices as reforestation and watershed protection, and suggested that the Adirondacks were a good laboratory for testing these ideas.

Another trend in the middle decades of the 19th century was an increasing acceptance of wilderness. This was brought about partly through the work of poets such as William Cullen Bryant, writers such as Henry David Thoreau, and artists such as Frederick Church. Also contributing to this trend was the fact that, as the frontier moved steadily westward, the wilderness was no longer seen as a physical threat, at least not in the more populous, affluent East.

Vacationers, tubercular patients, conservationists, wilderness devotees—all of these people wanted to see the resources of the Adirondacks preserved. This was partially achieved in 1885, when, after much political wrangling, the New York State legislature created the Adirondack Forest Preserve and directed that "the lands now or hereafter constituting the Forest Preserve shall be forever kept as wild forest lands." This action marked the first time a state government had set aside a significant piece of wilderness for reasons other than its scenic uniqueness.

In 1892, the legislature created the Adirondack State Park, consisting of Adirondack Forest Preserve land plus all privately owned land within a somewhat arbitrary boundary surrounding the Adirondacks, known as the "blue line" because it was drawn in blue on a large state map when it was first established. In 1894, in response to continuing abuses of the Forest Preserve law, the state's voters approved the inclusion of the "forever wild" portion of that law in the constitution of New York State, thus creating the only wilderness preserve in the nation that has constitutional protection.

Today the Forest Preserve consists of 2.3 million acres, being those lands owned by the people of the State of New York that are within the 6 million-acre Adirondack State Park, which is the largest park in the nation outside of Alaska.

In the first decade of the 20th century, raging fires consumed hundreds of thousands of acres of prime Adirondack forest lands; the scars from these fires can still be seen in many locations, both in exposed rock and in vegetation patterns. After World War I, tourism gradually took over as the primary industry in the Adirondacks. The arrival of the automobile, the invention of theme parks (some of the very first of which were in the Adirondacks), the development of winter sports facilities (with Lake Placid hosting the Winter Olympics in 1932), the increasing popularity of camping and hiking, and the growth of the second-home industry all brought such pressures to bear on the region that in 1968 Governor Nelson Rockefeller created a Temporary Study Commission on the Future of the Adirondacks. This commission made 181 recommendations, chief among them that a comprehensive land use plan, covering both public and private lands, be put in place and administered. This was accomplished by 1973, with the creation of the land use plans and the Adirondack Park Agency to manage them. While the plans and the Agency have remained controversial, they are indicative of the need to address the issues facing the Adirondacks boldly and innovatively.

In 1985, there were 112,000 permanent residents and 90,000 seasonal residents in the 9375-square-mile Adirondack Park, which is roughly the size of Vermont. Recreation, forestry, mining and agriculture are the principal industries in the Park.

The Southern Region

The trails described in this book are located in the southern region of the Adirondack Park. The area offers a variety of adventures over rolling or relatively level terrain. For this reason most trails, except for those in the mountainous eastern sections, are suitable for cross-country skiing.

The region is bounded to the north by NY Route 8, to the east by US Route 9, to the south by the "blue line" boundary of the Adirondack Park, and to the west by Hinckley Reservoir. The western areas are almost exclusively owned by private individuals and consist of farmland and wetlands.

Historically, the southern Adirondacks met much the same fate as the more northern sections, only several years earlier. The forests were stripped of their trees by the ravenous lumber and tanning industries at the beginning of the 19th century. Logging roads entered the interior, and temporary logging and mining settlements dotted the landscape for several years. The mining was mostly confined to red paint pigments, with the more lucrative minerals, such as garnet and iron, found farther north.

For the most part the area was unsuited for farming, with the rich, fertile valley of the Mohawk to the south and land to the west offering much better soil to grow crops. The soggy, rocky, logged-over forests of the southern Adirondacks had lost their value by the late 1800s; the state then acquired much of what is now the Wild Forest and Wilderness lands of the southern area.

Using This Guidebook

Like all the books in the Adirondack Mountain Club Forest Preserve Series of Guides to Adirondack Trails, this book is intended to be both a reference tool for planning trips and a field guide to carry on the trail. All introductory material should be read carefully, for it contains important information regarding the use of this book as well as numerous suggestions for safe and proper travel by foot in the Adirondacks. For campers, there is an important section on the relevant rules and regulations for camping in the Adirondacks.

The introduction to each section in this book will give hikers an idea of the varied opportunities available in the southern Adirondack region. There are many beautiful and seldom-visited places aside from the popular hiking, climbing and camping areas; this guide will help you find and explore these remote spots.

Nevertheless, trails are always changing, and despite the most careful preparation, any guidebook will, in time, develop inaccuracies. We encourage users of this guidebook to notify the Director of Publications, Adirondack Mountain Club, 174 Glen St., Glens Falls, NY 12801, of any errors, additions, or other changes that are needed. In doing so, users ensure that later editions will be as accurate as possible.

Maps

The map enclosed in the back of this book is a composite of U.S. Geological Survey quadrangles with updated overlays of trails, shelters and private land lines. These maps are especially valuable because of their combination of contour lines from the original base maps and recent trail information, updated with each printing of this guide. They cover most of the terrain described in this guidebook, but a few isolated trails not conveniently shown on them are shown on a page map on p. 142 Glasgow Mills. Extra copies of the southern region map are available from many retailers or directly from the Adirondack Mountain Club, 174 Glen St., Glens Falls, NY 12801.

Trail Signs and Markers

The routes described in this guidebook vary from wide, well-marked and frequently travelled DEC trails to narrow, unmarked footpaths used primarily by hunters and fishermen. Snowmobile trails are occasionally obscured in places by lush vegetation, but they can be discerned by checking for disks higher up on the trees, or by noting the relatively wide route tunneled through the trees and undergrowth.

Most routes in the southern region are isolated and, except for the popular mountains in the eastern section, the hiking group will most likely encounter no others on the trail. Thus hikers should never expect immediate help should an emergency occur. This is particularly true in winter when the unused, inviting, but trailless marshy areas of summer can be easily invaded by the skier or snowshoer.

With normal alertness, the trails in this region are easy to follow. In most cases, the beginning of the trail and trail junctions are marked. As far as possible, descriptions in this guidebook are detailed enough so that a hiker can find the correct route even in cases where trail signs are non-existent or temporarily missing. The trails themselves are usually marked with blue, yellow or red metal disks bearing the DEC insignia. Signboards are generally marked with destination and distances. Snowmobile trail markers have larger disks than hiking and ski trails, and generally are placed farther apart and higher.

Several trails described in this guidebook are unmarked, but hunters and fishermen use them frequently and keep them in excellent condition. An ''unmarked'' trail simply means that DEC is not officially maintaining it. Should a trail become unclear, one hiker should remain at the last known point of the trail, and the others fan out in all directions, keeping within sight and sound of each other until the continuation of the trail is located. Blowdowns or beaver activity are frequently the cause of a ''lost trail.''

A few trails in this guide are over private land, and are so noted. The trails are usually public rights of way, but there may be ''posted'' signs at some points. These are there to remind hikers that they are on private land over which the owner has kindly granted permission to pass. Leaving the trail or camping, fishing, and hunting are not permitted on these lands. Continued goodwill of public-spirited Adirondack landowners is dependent upon all hikers exercising respect and good judgment.

Distance and Time

All distances along the trails in this guidebook have been measured by a pedometer. Care has been taken to be as accurate as possible in determining distances, which are generally accurate to a tenth of a mile. DEC established distances on marked trails have been verified and noted in this guide if modification is necessary where obvious discrepancies occur.

At the start of each section is a list of trails in the area, the mileage unique to the trail, and the page number of the trail description. All mileage distances are cumulative, with the trail beginning at the 0 mi. point. A distance summary is given at the end of each trail description with the total distance expressed in miles and kilometers. To the inexperienced hiker, these distances will seem longer on the trail, as there is a great difference between ''sidewalk'' miles and ''trail'' miles. Moreover, old trail sign distances do not always reflect recent changes in trail routes or deviations for beaver ponds and blowdown avoidance. DEC has used a variety of measuring methods over the years and has not always updated every sign after every change of distance caused by rerouting, etc. In all cases where there is a disagreement, this guidebook can be assumed to be correct.

No attempt has been made to estimate travel times for these trails. A conservative rule to follow in estimating time is to allow an hour for every 1.5 mi., plus one-half hour for each 1000 ft. ascended. Experience will soon give each hiker an idea of how close his or her pace comes to this suggested standard. Most day hikers will probably hike faster, but backpackers will no doubt find they go more slowly.

Abbreviations and Conventions

In each book in the Forest Preserve Series, R and L, with periods omitted, are used for right and left. The R and L banks of a stream are determined by looking downstream. Likewise, the R fork of a stream is on the R when one faces downstream. N, S, E and W, again without periods, are used for north, south, east and west. The following abbreviations are used in the text and on the maps:

ADK	Adirondack Mountain Club
APA	Adirondack Park Agency
CCC	Civilian Conservation Corps (Depression Era)
DEC	New York State Department of Environmental Conservation
N-P	Northville-Placid (Trail)
USGS	United States Geological Survey
ft.	feet
km.	kilometer or kilometers
m.	meter or meters
mi.	mile or miles
yds.	yards

Wilderness Camping

It is not the purpose of this series to teach hikers how to camp in the woods. Many good books are available on that subject which are more comprehensive and useful than any information that could be given in the limited space available here. Hikers should be aware, however, of the differences and peculiarities of the Adirondacks. Currently recommended procedures to reduce environmental damage—particularly in heavily used areas—are outlined below.

Except for Johns Brook Lodge, 3.5 mi. up the Marcy Trail from Keene Valley (see *Guide to Adirondack Trails: High Peaks Region*), there are no huts in the Adirondacks for public use. There are, however, lean-tos at many convenient locations along the trails, and there are also numerous possibilities for tenting along the way. The regulations regarding tenting and the use of lean-tos are simple and unrestrictive when compared to those of other popular backpacking areas in the country; but it is important that every backpacker know and abide by the restrictions that do exist, since they are designed to promote the long-term enjoyment of the greatest number of people.

General Camping Guidelines:

Except for groups of ten or more (or smaller groups planning to spend more than three nights in one place), no camping or fire permits are required in the Adirondacks, but campers must obey all DEC regulations regarding camping. Listed below are some of the most important regulations. Complete regulations are available from the DEC and are posted at most access points.

1) No camping within 150 ft. of a stream, other water source, or trail except at designated campsites; other areas are designated with the following symbol:

2) Except in an emergency, no camping is permitted above 4000 ft. in elevation. (This rule does not apply from December 1 to April 30.)

3) All washing of dishes should be done at least 150 ft. from any stream, pond or other water source. **No soap**, even so-called "biodegradable" soap, should ever get into the water, so use a pot to carry water at least 150 ft. away from

your source and wash items and dispose of water there. One can also take a surprisingly effective bath by taking a quick dip and then using a pot for soaping and rinsing away from the stream or pond.

4) All human excrement **should be buried** under at least four inches of dirt at a spot at least 150 ft. away from any water source, and all toilet paper likewise buried or burned. Use established privies or latrines when available.

5) No wood except for **dead** and **down** timber may be used for fire building. Good wood is often scarce at popular campsites, so a stove is highly recommended.

6) No fire should be built near or on any flammable material. Much of the forest cover in the Adirondacks is composed of recently rotted twigs, leaves, or needles and is **highly flammable.** Build a fire at an established fireplace or on rocks or sand. Before leaving, destroy all traces of any new fireplace created.

7) All refuse must be completely burned or carried out of the woods. **Do not bury** any refuse and be sure that no packaging to be burned contains metal foil; it will not burn no matter how hot the fire. If you carried it in, you can carry it out again.

8) In general, leave no trace of your presence when leaving a campsite, and help keep the area clean and attractive by carrying out more than you carried in.

Lean-tos:

Lean-tos are available on a first-come, first-served basis up to the capacity of the shelter—usually about seven persons. A small party therefore cannot claim exclusive use of a shelter and must allow late arrivals equal use. Most lean-tos have a fireplace in front (sometimes with a primitive grill) and sanitary facilities. Most are located near some source of water, but each camper must use his own judgment as to whether or not the water supply needs purification before drinking.

It is in very poor taste to carve or write one's initials in a shelter. Please try to keep these rustic shelters in good condition and appearance.

Since reservations cannot be made for any of these shelters, it is best to carry a tent or other alternate shelter. Many shelters away from the standard routes, however, are rarely used and a small party can often find a shelter open in the more remote areas.

The following regulations apply specifically to lean-tos, in addition to the general camping regulations listed above:

1) No plastic may be used to close off the front of a shelter.
2) No nails or other permanent fastener may be used to affix a tarp in a lean-to, but it is permissible to use rope to tie canvas or nylon tarps across the front.
3) No tent may be pitched inside a lean-to.

Groups:

Any group of ten or more persons, or smaller groups planning to spend more than three nights in one place, must obtain a permit *before* camping on state land. This system is designed to prevent overuse of certain sites and also to encourage groups to split into smaller parties more in keeping with the natural environment. Permits can be obtained from the DEC forest ranger closest to the actual starting point of one's proposed trip. The local forest ranger can be contacted by writing to him directly; if in doubt about whom to write, send the letter to the Department of Environmental Conservation, Ray Brook, NY 12977. They will forward the letter, but allow at least a week for the letter to reach the appropriate forest ranger.

One can also make the initial contact with the forest ranger by phone, but keep in mind that rangers' schedules during the busy summer season are often unpredictable. Forest rangers are listed in the white pages of local phone books under "New York, State of; Environmental Conservation, Department of; Forest Ranger." Bear in mind when calling that most rangers operate out of their private homes, and observe the normal courtesy used when calling a private residence. Contact by letter is much preferred, and, as one can see, camping with a large group requires careful planning several weeks before the trip.

Drinking Water

For many years, hikers could trust practically any water source in the Adirondacks to be pure and safe to drink. Unfortunately, as in many other mountain areas, some Adirondack water sources have become contaminated with a parasite known as *Giardia lamblia*. This intestinal parasite causes a disease known as Giardiasis—often called "Beaver Fever." It can be spread by any warm-blooded mammal when infected feces wash into the water; beavers are prime agents in transferring this parasite because they spend so much of their time in and near the water. Hikers themselves have also become primary agents in spreading this disease since some individuals appear to be unaffected carriers, and other recently infected individuals may inadvertently spread the parasite before their symptoms become apparent.

Prevention: Follow the guidelines for the disposal of human excrement as stated in the "Wilderness Camping" section of this guide. Equally important, make sure every member of your group is aware of the problem and follows the guidelines as well. The health of a fellow hiker may depend on you.

Choosing a Water Source: While no water source can be guaranteed to be safe, smaller streams high in the mountains, which have no possibility of a beaver dam or temporary human presence upstream, are usually safe to drink. If there is any doubt, treat the water before drinking it.

Treatment: Boil all water 3 minutes, administer an iodine-based chemical purifier (available at camping supply stores and some drug and department stores), or use a commercial filter designed specifically for Giardiasis prevention. If after returning from a trip you experience recurrent intestinal problems, consult your physician and explain your potential problem.

Forest Safety

The southern Adirondacks are primarily rolling or flat terrain covered with a mixture of deciduous and evergreen forests, dotted with many lakes and marshes. The eastern portion includes several smaller mountain ridges which, while not as rugged as the High Peaks, are nevertheless potentially hazardous with steep ascents, cliffs and open summits. Several with the most spectacular views and scenic ridges can be reached only by bushwhacking using a map and compass.

In summer the day hiker should take reasonable care: carry extra clothing, rain poncho, food and water, and have confidence and reasonable knowledge—at least prior map consultation—of the trails being explored, and an awareness of the weather.

Off-trail hiking, or bushwhacking, is not to be undertaken lightly. Special preparations should be made. Make minimal preparations to bivouac overnight should the group misjudge time and distances or become disoriented and lost. Know how to read a map and compass before starting, or be sure at least two group members are experienced off-trail hikers. Bushwhacking requires an ability to read the land and to judge distances, both of which come only with experience. In the beginning, caution, conservative judgment of the time necessary to complete the trip, and reasonable care should result in a successful trip.

Winter trips should be carefully planned. Travel over ice on cross-country skiing trips must be approached with caution. The possibility of freezing rain, snow and cold temperatures should always be considered from early September until late May. True winter conditions can commence as early as November and last into April. In winter especially, never ski or snowshoe with fewer than four persons in the party. Take care that each person's equipment and clothing are adequate for conditions, rest as necessary, and drink plenty of water. For more information on winter travel, refer to the Adirondack Mountain Club publication *Winter Hiking and Camping* by John Danielsen.

Emergency Procedures

An ounce of prevention is always worth a pound of cure, but if one is in need of emergency assistance, the DEC forest rangers are the first people to contact for help. The names and phone numbers of the local rangers are often posted inside each trail register. Forest rangers are listed in the white pages of the local phone book under "New York, State of: Environmental Conservation, Department of; Forest Ranger." If this fails, try (during business hours) DEC headquarters in Ray Brook, NY: (518) 891-1370. The third place to try is the New York State Police division headquarters nearest the area in which the emergency has occurred. They will assist in contacting the persons best able to help. See that the person sent for help has the correct location of the emergency and a complete *written* description of the condition of any injured person before leaving for help.

Off-Trail Hiking

Several mountains in the eastern area of the southern region of the Adirondacks have spectacular views and no trails to the summit. These mountains are described in this guide with compass directions, using magnetic N as the base, and tips on the best way to get to the top. Compass *bearings* are not given, since each bushwhack will require a slightly different bearing, depending upon the starting point, the amount of deviation the hikers make L or R to avoid obstacles such as beaver dams, blowdown, swamps, cliffs, etc. Make allowance, when referring back to the map, for a magnetic declination of approximately 13 degrees W in this region. The time of year is often a factor in a successful bushwhack, since fall and early spring (before and after the foliage seasons) permit sight bearings to be made frequently and accurately.

Off-trail hiking should NEVER be done alone. Many sections of the southern region are wild and isolated, and should an injury or other emergency occur, the off-trail hiker cannot depend upon being "found" by other hikers. Learn to read the map and compass and, through experience, to judge distances and time on a bushwhack. Watch the topography of the terrain and frequently check what is seen against the map topography. Learn from experienced bushwhackers, if possible, and if not, assemble at least four persons and take short trips to known destinations before attempting a longer, trailless mountain.

Canoe Routes

Numerous lakes in the southern region make it an ideal destination for canoeists. One of the most popular routes is to canoe downstream along the West Branch of the Sacandaga from Arietta at the S end to Shaker Place, the former site of the Shaker farm. There are now no obvious signs of the farm; instead there is a sandy clearing used as a parking area 3.5 mi. N of Avery's Hotel. As the river flows S to N the ideal trip is to put-in at the parking area along NY 10, next to the second bridge that crosses it on NY 10. The approximately 7 mi. canoe trip through the swampy valley is a delightful day's outing in the warmer seasons.

A second short but interesting canoe trip is to paddle S (upstream) from the second bridge and take the first R into the outlet of Good Luck Lake, canoeing for approximately 1.0 mi. into lovely Good Luck Lake. There are several primitive campsites along its shores, accessible only by boat. (See Canada Lake, Caroga Lake and Powley-Piseco Road Section for a description of the hiking trail into Good Luck Lake.)

West Lake's state fishing access site off West Lake Road provides canoeists and other boaters a route into West, Canada and Lily Lakes for a day's exploration of those areas. (See *Adirondack Canoe Waters—South and West Flow* published by ADK.)

The Adirondack Mountain Club

The Adirondack Mountain Club (or ADK, the initials AMC having been claimed by the previously formed Appalachian Mountain Club) was organized in 1922 for the purpose of bringing together in a working unit a large number of people interested in the mountains, trails, camping, and forest conservation. A permanent club headquarters was established, and with increasing membership, club chapters were organized. The chapters are as follows: Adirondak Loj (North Elba), Albany, Algonquin (Plattsburgh), Black River (Watertown), Cold River (Long Lake), Finger Lakes (Ithaca-Elmira), Genesee Valley (Rochester), Glens Falls, Hurricane Mt. (Keene), Iroquois (Utica), Keene Valley, Knickerbocker (New York City), Lake Placid, Laurentian (Canton-Potsdam), Long Island, Mid-Hudson

(Poughkeepsie), Mohican (Westchester Co.), New York, Niagara Frontier (Buffalo), North Jersey (Bergen Co., NJ), North Woods (Saranac Lake-Tupper Lake), Onondaga (Syracuse), Penn's Woods (Harrisburg, PA), Ramapo (Pearl River), Schenectady, Shatagee Woods (Malone), and Susquehanna (Oneonta). In addition, there is an extensive membership-at-large.

Most chapters do not have qualifying requirements; a note to the membership coordinator, Adirondack Mountain Club, 174 Glen St., Glens Falls, NY 12801, will bring you information on membership in a local chapter (e.g. names and addresses of persons to be contacted) or details on membership-at-large. Persons joining a chapter, upon payment of their chapter dues, *ipso facto* become members of the club. Membership dues include a subscription to *Adirondac*, a 10-times-yearly magazine, and discounts on ADK books and at ADK lodges. An application for membership is in the back of this book.

Members of the Adirondack Mountain Club have formulated the following creed, which reflects the theme of the club and its membership:

I support the Club's work to insure that the lands of the State constituting the Forest Preserve shall be forever kept as wild forest lands in accordance with Article XIV, Section 1, of the New York State Constitution. I wish to be part of the Club's volunteer-based conservation, education and recreation activities aimed at protecting the Forest Preserve and encouraging outdoor recreation, consistent with its wild forest character.

In the 1980s ten thousand-plus "ADKers" enjoy the full spectrum of outdoor activities including hiking, backpacking, canoeing (from floating on a pond to whitewater racing), rock climbing, cross-country skiing and snowshoeing. Most chapters have an active year-round outings schedule as well as regular meetings and programs featuring individuals ranging from chapter members to local and state officials. Many ADKers are also active in service work ranging from participation in search-and-rescue organizations to involvement in the ongoing debate over the best use of our natural resources and forest or wilderness lands, not only in the Adirondacks but in their immediate localities as well.

Adirondack Mountain Club Lodges

The Adirondack Mountain Club, Inc. owns and operates two lodges for overnight guests in the High Peaks region. Johns Brook Lodge is accessible only by foot, while Adirondak Loj can be reached by car.

Johns Brook Lodge:

Johns Brook Lodge (JBL) is on the trail to Mt. Marcy, 5.12 mi. from Keene Valley and 3.52 mi. from the trailhead at the Garden. The lodge is open daily to all comers for meals and lodging from mid-June until Labor Day (during which it has a resident staff) and on weekends from Memorial Day Weekend until late June and the weekend after Labor Day until Columbus Day (on a caretaker basis). During the summer season, the hutmaster in charge will make every effort to accommodate transients, but only reservations in advance will guarantee space in one of the two bunkrooms. Available all year long in the immediate vicinity of JBL are other accommodations owned by the Adirondack Mountain Club, Inc.: 3 lean-tos, and 2 cabins with cooking facilities—Winter Camp (housing 12), and Grace Camp (housing 6). For further details and reservation information, contact Johns Brook Lodge, c/o Adirondak Loj, P.O. Box 867, Lake Placid, NY 12946 (telephone: 518/523-3441).

Adirondak Loj:

This facility (the unusual spelling stems from the phonetic spelling system of Melvil Dewey, founder of the Lake Placid Club, which built the original structure) is 9 mi. by car from the village of Lake Placid. In addition to the Loj, the Adirondack Mountain Club owns the square mile of surrounding property, including all of Heart Lake and most of Mt. Jo. The Loj offers accommodations to all comers by the day or week, all year long, either in private bedrooms or in bunkrooms. Other accommodations include cabins, lean-tos with fireplaces, and numerous tent sites, for which nominal charges are made. Basic camping supplies may be purchased at the High Peaks Information Center building located at the entrance to the parking lot at the Loj. A nominal parking charge is made for nonmembers not registered at the Loj or using the lean-tos or tent sites.

Several cross-country ski trails are located on the property and on nearby Forest Preserve land. This extensive network is a center of much wintertime activity. Snowshoers find much territory in which to enjoy their particular sport.

Of special interest at Adirondak Loj is a Nature Museum where one may find specimens of mosses, lichens, birds' nests, rocks and other items from the natural world. A modest library is available to help those who wish to identify their own samples.

A ranger-naturalist program is offered during the summer months. The leader conducts walks along marked nature trails and arranges talks and slide programs on nature and conservation topics. The latter are generally conducted in a scenic outdoor amphitheatre especially constructed for this purpose.

For full information about reservations, rates or activities, write to the Manager, Adirondak Loj, P.O. Box 867, Lake Placid, NY 12946 (telephone: 518/523-3441).

NEAL S. BURDICK, Forest Preserve Series Editor
LINDA LAING, Author, *Guide to Adirondack Trails: Southern Region*

STONY CREEK, HADLEY AND THE EASTERN SECTION

The most easterly section of the southern area of the Park is bordered by US 9 to the E, NY 28 to the NE, and NY 8 to the N. These highways, in addition to the Adirondack Northway (I-87), grant relatively easy access to some of the most attractive, seldom visited mountains in the Park.

Although most of the lands in this section are privately owned, many of the mountains are accessible using state trails or bushwhacking through unposted land. They are well worth climbing for their rugged scenery and windswept, bare summits, a legacy of the forest fires at the turn of the century. Lumber companies had stripped most of the trees, and the dry slash they left burned fiercely when ignited by lightning or the sparks from a passing railroad engine. Rains and melting snows subsequently washed much of the thin soil from the rocky mountaintops. Today lichens, mosses and mountain berries grow there in undisturbed carpets of jewel-like green, red and yellow.

The forested slopes have largely recovered, and provide attractive routes for the hiker. Four of the loveliest mountains in this section are trailless and must be climbed with caution—and always with a topographic map and compass. (See Introduction for more information on bushwhacking.)

Recommended hikes include the following:

SHORT HIKES:

Hadley Mt.—1.8 mi. A short but rewarding climb to a bare summit with a manned fire tower.

Prospect Mt.—1.4 mi. Walk the historic cog railway bed to the summit and gain a sense of history as well as super views.

MODERATE HIKES:

Paint Mine Ruins—2.3 mi. A path traverses a wild valley using an old, overgrown road to the site of a former mine and outbuildings where paint pigments were once mined and dried.

Crane Mt—1.4 mi. This spectacular mountain can be hiked up one side and descended on the other, with a visit to Crane Mt. Pond along the way, to make an adventure filled loop back to the parking lot. (Loop distance 4.1 mi.)

HARDER HIKES:

Baldhead Mt. and Moose Mt.—3.6 mi. (approximate). Bushwhack to a pristine pair of neighbors, each offering super views from bare, rocky summits.

Huckleberry Mt—2.5 mi. (approximate). Bushwhack to the top of a long, windswept ridge with extraordinary scenery.

HADLEY MT.

Some of the most spectacular views in the southern Adirondacks are obtained by hiking to the bare summit of Hadley Mt. And, although it is one of the few remaining mountains in the state with a manned fire tower (1986), one need not climb the tower to be rewarded. Hadley is the tallest of the three peaks that form West Mt. Ridge and is open to views in three directions.

To reach the trailhead, take NY 9N to the village of Lake Luzerne, then go N on Stony Creek Road (which is route 1) from the village approximately 3 mi. to Hadley Hill Road. Turn W (L) and drive up Hadley Hill Road. Proceed 4.6 mi. to Tower Road, which is marked with a road sign, the second major R off Hadley Hill Road. Turn N onto Tower Road (dirt) and drive for another 1.5 mi. to the trailhead on the L where a rocky clearing will accommodate several cars. (Tower Road is usually in very good driving condition for normal passenger cars, although in early spring there may be some muddy areas and rocky washouts.)

The entire West Mt. Ridge and much of the surrounding forests were burned over in 1903, 1908, 1911, and again in 1915. A rusted iron sign, erected in 1936, reminds the visitor of this sad history.

The trail begins to the W (L) of the parking area and immediately climbs a moderate grade, traversing a washed-out old jeep trail. Although the trail is well marked with red DEC trail markers, it is very easy to follow due to severe erosion as well as a good deal of use by hikers. Several sections have been worn down to bedrock, including an attractive area at 0.3 mi. that resembles a slanted city sidewalk. In other areas large rocks and boulders have been revealed to create an obstacle course for the climber.

Climbing continues through predominantly hardwood forest for the first mile, except for the very beginning where the trail passes through a mature stand of hemlocks. The general direction is W, and the trail climbs steadily upward at a moderate pitch. There is a brief flat section where a small stream is crossed at 0.5 mi. Here an attractive, large boulder makes a good resting place.

After crossing the stream, the trail bends slightly R and continues to climb. At 0.6 mi. rock formations can be seen on the R. These are 10 to 15 ft. high; while attractive in summer, they are noted in winter for their colorful blue-green ice formations.

Finally, a much steeper section of the trail culminates at the top of a ridge at 1.0 mi. A turn L begins a gentle section across the top of this rib of West Mt. Ridge. This is a lovely part of the trail, open and most welcome after the moderately steep but relentless climb.

At 1.2 mi. after a brief upward grade, a swing L occurs and the trail passes through a grove of stunted, picturesque trees consisting of oak, mountain ash, maple, and birch, among others. Now headed in a NW direction, at 1.3 mi. the trail jogs R and begins a moderate climb up the next ridge.

Cliffs rise on either side as the trail continues upward through the col. At 1.3 mi. a clearing is reached, which is used as the observer's supply vehicle turnaround. Here the trail branches to the L and also continues straight ahead. Each route leads to the summit, but the best trail for pre-summit views, and thus the most popular, is to the L.

Taking the L fork, climbing continues at a moderate rate of ascent until at 1.4 mi. the trail reaches the first of a series of lookouts—a spectacular view of Great Sacandaga Lake. For the remaining 0.3 mi. the trail circles the L (SW) side of Hadley, traversing several open areas that grant the hiker marvelous vistas. At 1.7 mi., after the last rocky outlook has been passed, the trail levels briefly, then splits again with the the R fork going 200 ft. to the observer's cabin and the L making a slight climb to the summit, which is reached at 1.8 mi. Here, on a clear day, the successful climber enjoys a brilliant panorama, an ample reward for the effort expended.

In addition to Great Sacandaga Lake to the S and Spruce Mt. to the W, one can see from the summit Crane, Mt. Blue, Moose, Baldhead, and Pharaoh mountains, as well as Lake Champlain—and on a very clear day several of the High Peaks.

The adventurous group with a map and compass can continue this hike by bushwhacking from the summit of Hadley Mt. to the summit of Roundtop Mt. to the N (see below). Roundtop can be sighted from Hadley's tower; it is a small mountain with a bare summit and a pristine quality of peaceful isolation and unspoiled natural beauty.

Distances: To rock formations, 0.6 mi.; to West Mt. Ridge, 1.0 mi.; to summit, 1.8 mi. (2.9 km.). Ascent 1525 ft. (466 m.). Elevation 2675 ft. (818 m.).

ROUNDTOP MT.

BUSHWHACK

Roundtop Mt. is an explorer's delight, a fairly easy bushwhack adventurous hikers can do to extend the trip up Hadley Mt. Both Hadley and Roundtop would be tied in the contest for ''most picturesque'' of the bare summit peaks in the southern Adirondacks. A trip to Roundtop's pristine and infrequently visited bald summit will leave a taste for more of the same. The orange berries of mountain ash and green-gray lichens and mosses against bare summit rocks provide plenty of colorful scenery as well as interesting mountain-top nature study subjects.

To reach this delightful mountain, climb Hadley Mt. first (see above). From Hadley's fire tower one sees Roundtop to the NNE, its bare face inviting a visit. With compass and topographic map, begin walking N through the stunted undergrowth; bear a bit to the W to encounter bare rocks almost immediately. These rocky faces provide plenty of attractive scenery and easy walking, but it is frequently necessary to enter the scrub and tangled undergrowth.

Take care not to begin a steep descent to the E or W, but keep to the crest of the ridge as it continues in a northerly direction towards Roundtop. Just before the descent into the col, views of Roundtop can be glimpsed through the trees. This is the time to recheck the compass direction and take a second bearing (which should be almost the same as that taken from the tower).

Begin to descend approximately 400 ft. into the col between the two mountains after going about 1.0 mi. from Hadley's summit. Continue through the attractive open hardwood forest across the small valley to the foot of Roundtop; as the ascent begins, a line of rugged cliffs is encountered. These, however, can be negotiated through several crevices and cracks. The climbing is sometimes rather steep. A second cliff line before the summit can easily be skirted by going to the L or R, where, after a scramble up and over several large boulders, the summit is attained.

There are views in every direction. On a clear day, several High Peaks can be sighted and identified to the N, in addition to nearby Crane, Baldhead and Moose Mts.

The easiest way to return is to go back across the ridge to Hadley, but the experienced bushwhacking group may elect the adventure of descending the E slope and turning S to intersect Tower Road. In previous years it was possible merely to descend E straight into the valley and intersect Wolf Creek Road, then turn R and have an easy and pleasant walk out to Tower Road, making an interesting loop back to the Hadley parking area. Recently the owners of Roundtop have logged the lower slopes of the E side, leaving large sections of tangled briars and heavy undergrowth with slippery branches and scrap logs hidden underneath.

To avoid this impossibly difficult section, the hiker should descend carefully, avoiding the cliffs by angling NE, and then turning SE until the lumbered sections are sighted, staying above them by continuing due S and bushwhacking directly back to Tower Road. Turn W (R) when the road is reached and walk back to the parking area. This loop route is now difficult and requires careful attention to the map and compass. It will help to have acquired the ability to read the land in order to decide how far to go in each direction and when to turn to avoid the cliffs and the worst of the underbrush.

Distances: To summit of Hadley Mt., 1.8 mi.; to summit of Roundtop Mt., 2.6 mi. (4.2 km.) (approximate). Elevation, 2400 ft. (732 m.).

BALDHEAD MT. AND MOOSE MT.

BUSHWHACK LOOP TREK OVER TWO OPEN PEAKS

Baldhead Mt. and Moose Mt. are two of the most delightful mountains in the southern Adirondacks. Open views and dazzling rocky cliffs and ledges provide the adventurous hiker with magnificent rewards for the risk. And the risk is minimal, since each mountain is easy to locate and climb. A loop trip is possible, and recommended, since climbing Baldhead first and then going across the ridge connecting the two mountains takes advantage of the elevation already gained.

Drive N on Harrisburg Road from the village of Stony Creek, turn R on Tucker Road and continue to the height of land where there is a parking turnout on the R. Park here and begin the climb on the L (N) side of the road, bushwhacking through a stand of beech trees where numerous young beech saplings make the going somewhat difficult.

Travel over a small knoll that tops out at approximately 0.6 mi. and then descends quickly into a col. Now begin climbing a much larger knoll. Note on the R very bright yellow paint slashes on various trees, which mark the boundary line between state and private land. The E side of this boundary shows signs of logging in the past few years, so staying to the W of the yellow boundary markers will make the walking much easier. The hiker can easily follow the paint blazes to the top of this knoll.

Continue heading due N to reach the crest at 1.0 mi. The top is flat and has some attractive rock slabs decorated with lichen, mosses and blueberries. Limited views are available to the S and N where Baldhead can now be seen.

Continue N and descend a steep grade down approximately 250 ft. to cross a small stream at the bottom and begin the actual climb up the flank of Baldhead. A series of open rock areas provides easy walking and several views to the S and W.

At 1.9 mi. a larger open rock area begins. This often gets quite steep, yet affords ample rocky resting places. Some sandstone boulders can be found here, and blueberries, mountain ash, and many varieties of moss and lichens crackle and crunch underfoot.

The last quarter mile to the summit is quite steep, but there are plenty of grassy sections, interspersed with shrubs and slabs of flat rock, lending a special beauty to this untrammeled place.

At approximately 2.2 mi. the summit is reached. There are several bald areas, and beautiful thickets of spruce and hemlock, stunted white birch and twisted cherry and mountain ash. Views to the N are excellent and show the S cliffs of Crane Mt. in their rocky splendor. To the E, and seemingly very near, is Moose Mt. with its dramatic bare rock expanses.

To continue on to Moose, head NE and descend to the flat ridge, which is covered with scrubby spruce and balsam and numerous small white paper birch trees. At the end of the ridge, descend into the col briefly, then begin the climb up Moose Mt. The ascent of Moose also provides numerous rocky outlooks and bare stretches of rock slabs that are easily climbed. The summit of Moose is approximately 1.4 mi. from the summit of Baldhead.

The large, bare summit is outstanding, with a balancing rock, spruce and mountain ash, and many, many open rock areas upon which to sit and enjoy the scenery.

To return, descend in a S direction, keeping to the open rocks as much as possible and avoiding the deep ravine to the W. Since there are periodic ravines and cliffs to the E also, descending more or less on top of the open ridge is easiest and leads directly to the private road that parallels Twin Brooks, which in turn leads back to Tucker Road.

As the road comes in sight, a silver trailer parked at its end is easy to spot. A beaver dam is to the W (R) of the road, and the hiker need only walk downhill now approximately 1.0 mi., back to Tucker Road and R about a quarter mile to the car.

Although this dirt road is privately maintained by the Gill, DeLorenzo and Hartz families as well as the Bit and Bridle Ranch, Dominick DeLorenzo advises that hikers are welcome to walk it anytime. Do not try to drive on it, however, without permission—and a four-wheel-drive vehicle.

Distances: To top of knoll, 1.0 mi.; to Baldhead summit, 2.2 mi. (3.6 km.); to Moose summit from Baldhead, 1.4 mi.; (from road, 3.6 mi.) (5.8 km.).

Huckleberry Mt.

HUCKLEBERRY MT.

BUSHWHACK

One of the most scenic little mountains in the southern Adirondacks, Huckleberry Mt. is privately owned, except for the NW corner and the top, but at present (1987) is unposted. Permission may be required, however, at some time in the future.

At 2435 ft. it is not among the highest, but for sheer beauty and the windswept drama of a mile and a half of spectacular ridge walking, it cannot be equaled. Huckleberry's S and SW face is a series of spectacular cliffs. Although it can be climbed from that side by carefully choosing a route up a draw, it is far safer and easier to climb from the NW end, utilizing the same state parking area where one begins the walk into the valley between Crane and Huckleberry that contains the ruins of the old paint mine (see below).

To reach the parking area, take NY 8 to Johnsburg and turn S on South Johnsburg Road. Drive 1.1 mi. and turn R on Hudson Street. Proceed another 2.3 mi. The parking area is on the S (L) side bordered by a rail fence and is large enough for several vehicles. It is the same parking area used for the trail to the Paint Mine Ruins referenced above.

Take the logging road that enters to the R of the parking lot—do not cross Paintbed Brook, but rather turn L onto the dirt logging road and parallel the brook for a short distance. At 0.1 mi. after a short uphill, a large clearing is entered. To the R about 500 yds. is a rudimentary camp with a shaded picnic area and tepee, but the hiker should continue along the road until at 0.3 mi. a short uphill section begins. Proceed up and through a large wet area and to a fork that cuts to the R at 0.4 mi. Take this R and shortly the lumber slash area filled with lush brambles and stinging nettles comes into view at 0.5 mi. To avoid this difficult section turn off the road here and into the forest to the S (R), and begin the ascent of Huckleberry up a draw through towering hemlocks.

The climbing is steep in places; soon ledges are encountered. They can be skirted either L or R or, more often, a way can be found through cracks and draws to go up and over them. Continue S and up, climbing steadily, sometimes steeply, until the first plateau is reached and the character of the forest changes from hemlock to the lovely, picturesque red pine. Continue S, angling a bit to the E, and soon the top of the cliffs will begin to offer outstanding bare ledges and rock outcroppings with views into the valley and mountains beyond. Climbing continues for a time, but the views give ample rewards for the efforts.

Twisted red pines against the rocky ledges, the soft greens and grays of lichens and moss, blueberries and bearberries, and the mountain-loving white three-toothed cinquefoil whose leaves turn deep red in the fall combine to create a wild and pristine ambiance. At any time of year, a walk along the ridge is one outstanding scene after another. A rare experience—this is a mountain quite unlike any other in the Adirondacks. It is not so much what is seen from the top, but what is seen all around on the top that is exquisitely lovely.

The entire round trip and exploration of the ridge is approximately 5.0 mi. in length and involves a climb of over 1000 ft. On the return trip, be sure to stay above the lumbered section by retracing the route used going up as nearly as possible. Blundering downhill too directly will require forcing one's way through incredible tangles of tall brambles, nettles, vines, and man-high shrubs—plus coping with hidden pitfalls consisting of deep ruts and discarded slash left on the forest floor by the lumbering operations of three or four years ago. It will take the forest another 10 to 15 years to recover sufficiently to permit easy passage by humans in any season but winter.

Distances: (Approximate) To first lookouts, 1.0 mi.; to top of ridge, 1.5 mi.; to end of ridge summit, 2.5 mi. (4.1 km.). Elevation, 2435 ft. (732 m.)

PAINT MINE RUINS

A visit to the old Paint Mine Ruins is an easy and attractive walk to the site of a most interesting historical ruin, now almost completely reclaimed by the forest. This walk offers something for the history buff as well as the nature lover.

The valley between Crane and Huckleberry Mts. in the mid- and late 1800s was the site of a flourishing paint mine that produced a dark red paint used locally to color barns and other buildings. Here the earth yielded an iron and aluminum pigment in great abundance for a time. The pits and foundations of several buildings can still be found.

To reach the trailhead, take NY 8 to Johnsburg and turn S on South Johnsburg Road. Proceed 1.1 mi. and turn R (W) on Hudson Street. Continue another 2.3 mi. to a parking area on the L (S) bordered by a rail fence and large enough for several vehicles.

Do not take the first dirt road next to the parking area unless the goal is to bushwhack up Huckleberry Mt. (see above). Walk the main paved road for 0.1 mi., crossing the bridge over Paintbed Brook, and continue up a small incline where another dirt road begins to the L (S). Turn onto this road. Although it appears to be driveable for regular automobiles for the first 0.1 mi. or so, it soon becomes extremely rough and accessible only to those with four-wheel-drive vehicles. Please note that although the land is not currently posted, it is privately owned and subject to restrictions at any time.

Reaching the top of the hill at 0.2 mi., the road forks L and a less traveled fork continues straight ahead. Bear L and continue a moderate climb up the washed-out road. At 0.5 mi. there is a narrow cutoff to the R over a log corduroy; ignore this and continue along the main road until a large grassy clearing appears on the L at 0.6 mi.

This clearing was obviously a staging area for lumber operations several years ago. At least three overgrown logging roads depart from the S side—a careful check shows that the center one has a well-worn path that continues down a small dip and then over the ridge in the distance. Take this path. It is **not marked,** but the woods are relatively open, consisting of a variety of hardwoods, and even in midsummer the path is evident for the entire way. It may, however, be obscured briefly by an occasional patch of berries or nettles. The direction is generally S, then SE, except for occasional twists and turns to avoid obstacles.

The path hugs the shoulder of Crane Mt. for a little over a mile to avoid the ravine created by Paintbed Brook, following faithfully the track of the old road. It climbs moderately at 1.1 mi. through a wet area and then jogs slightly R, going SSW paralleling Paintbed Creek on the L. At l.15 mi. the trail crosses a brook and skirts the shoulder of Crane Mt. Another small creek is crossed at 1.2 mi. A new path has been trampled to the R at 1.3 mi. to avoid a huge fallen tree.

The trail crosses a small tributary of Paintbed Creek at 1.4 mi. on a precarious log bridge. A few orange blazes can be seen on trees in this area, but they are not extensive enough to depend upon as trail markers for any distance. A wet area is crossed at 1.7 mi. and then a short climb to the top of a ridge begins. The ridge crest is reached at 1.8 mi. Several enormous erratics will be seen on the L at 1.9 mi. Some of these are as large as a two-to-three story building. They make very interesting subjects to explore.

Continuing along the now quite overgrown path, the old Paint Mine settlement is reached at 2.3 mi. The ruins become evident first on the L. Explore this area to see evidence of old buildings and the paint mine itself. The area can be identified initially by the presence of numerous young saplings that are rapidly filling in the clearing. Proceed E along the trail, then ESE to locate the paint pit on the R.

To the L are stone foundations with large birch trees sprouting from and surrounding them. Look to the R for the paint drying area, and circle E to locate an old stone chimney still standing upright. The mine is reported to have produced paint into the early 1900s.

Distances: To large grassy clearing, 0.6 mi.; to large erratics, 1.9 mi.; to ruins, 2.3 mi. (3.7 km.).

CRANE MT.

The most interesting, most used and most appreciated mountain in the southern Adirondacks is undoubtedly Crane Mt. It is unsurpassed for super views, luscious blueberries, and scenic side trails to explore. Two approaches to the summit make it possible to do a wonderful loop trip up, across the summit, and down the other side, exploring Crane Mt. Pond and the E ridge as well as the top where the abandoned tower still stands.

To reach the trailhead take Garnet Lake Road from the hamlet of Thurman (off S. Johnsburg Road). Proceed 1.4 mi. to a R turn marked with a DEC yellow and brown trail sign pointing the way to Crane Mt. The next section of road is dirt and may be rough going, especially in spring. It is maintained, however, and one need not have a four-wheel-drive—just caution.

Continue to the top of a long hill for 2.0 mi. and turn where a smaller dirt road cuts off to the R. For the next 0.6 mi. the road is difficult and sometimes partially flooded by beaver. Hikers may wish to park on the shoulder right before this last turn and walk the extra half-mile to the parking area and the beginning of the trailhead.

The parking area can accommodate at least a dozen cars. Walk L 20 ft. from the N end to locate the trail register and the beginning of both trails to the summit. The trail sign indicates 1.8 mi to the summit to the R (about 0.4 mi. more than it really is);1.4 mi. to Crane Mt.

Pond; 1 mi. to Putnam Junction; and 1.9 mi. to the pond taking the L route.

Taking the shortest route to the summit, the R fork, the trail goes through pleasant hardwoods and begins a moderate ascent at 0.1 mi. At 0.2 mi. one must negotiate a group of boulders. The first cliff face appears on the R at 0.3 mi., after which the trail levels off.

Following the contour of the side of the mountain only briefly, the trail now becomes steeper. A very steep section commences at 0.4 mi. On the R are more sheer rock faces and perhaps a small cave can be seen, but the cliff is too steep to attempt an investigation without rock climbing experience and proper equipment.

A level section occurs at 0.5 mi. A path goes L to bare rock and a lookout. At 0.6 mi. the trail hooks around a few pine trees and goes a bit R, then up and L over a bare rock expanse. The general direction here is NE. Cross the rock face N to the pines to find the continuation of the trail.

A junction is reached at 0.7 mi. A sign pointing R indicates 0.8 mi. to the summit. Take the R fork. (The L goes through a cool ravine to reach the pond in another 0.4 mi.) At 0.8 mi. climb a short, rustic ladder that has been placed against a long rock extrusion, which created a small cliff without hand or foot holds. The trail now turns L and continues through a flat area and a stand of fragrant balsam trees. Hemlocks, too, are in abundance as the trail continues along the ridge.

At 1.1 mi. the climbing begins again and at 1.2 mi. a longer ladder provides a means to ascend a very rugged cliff face. Reaching the top of this cliff, the trail bends R and the hiker scrambles over some large boulders to reach the rocks of the summit at 1.4 mi.

The tower is not in good repair and cannot be climbed. However, views to the S and SW are magnificent. To the S one can identify Mt. Blue, Hadley, Moose and Baldhead with little difficulty. Looking NW, on a clear day, Snowy Mt. and Indian Lake can be seen.

Continuing NW across the summit, the trail meanders in and out of the stubby, wind-bent evergreens, descending gently. At 1.7 mi. there is a fork L to a look-out with a great view of Crane Mt. Pond. Just after this wonderful lookout, the descent begins W and down a very steep section. At 2.3 mi. the trail levels off for about 500 yds. and then begins a more gentle descent to the pond. At 2.4 mi. a marshy spot must be negotiated. Very shortly thereafter a junction is reached. The path to the R leads to a popular camping area, while the L fork circles the pond.

The pond is popular with campers and fishermen. There are several overused camping areas along the shore. Despite this it is a lovely jewel of a lake with beaver and ducks and super scenery.

The hiker can continue around the pond and descend along the marked W trail, or take the trail E through the ravine where a small inlet stream runs into the E end of the lake. The E trail retraces part of the route used for the ascent. All the trails are well marked and well used. There is much to explore, including a bushwhack of the smaller W summit (see below).

Distances: To first lookout, 0.5 mi.; to junction, 0.7 mi.; to summit and tower, 1.4 mi. (2.3 km.); Ascent 1154 ft. (353 m.); Elevation 3254 ft.; (995 m.).

CRANE MT. POND AND NW RIDGE

PARTIAL BUSHWHACK

A second route to ascend Crane Mt. is on the SW side. It leads first to the pond, then around it to the R (E) and up again to the summit. Hikers who want to explore a little-visited section with bare rock faces and good views to the N and W can bushwhack across the NW rib of the mountain. The climb can be combined with a loop to the

main summit and back down the E trail (see above for directions to
the trailhead).

It would be wise to consider parking on the side of the access road
and not take the R turn on the tiny dirt road which leads 0.5 mi. into
the parking lot at the base of the trailhead. There is often standing
water due to beaver activity at one point, and deep ruts in two places.

However, the NW ridge hiker need only walk the road for 0.3 mi.
and take the L fork, which leads into the forest and is marked with a
bright yellow DEC ski trail disk. The main road continues another
0.2 mi. to the parking lot and the trail register, where the hiker could
also begin and take the L path from the trail register. That trail
connector returns to this marked ski/hiking trail, which is the old,
now overgrown, road to the Putnam Farm.

This old farm road leads downhill in a very gentle incline. At 0.5
mi. a small brook is crossed and remains on the L until the trail forks
at 0.7 mi. The cutoff R (W) is the trail to the pond and summit. Here
a sign says Crane Mt. Pond 0.9 mi. and Crane Mt. Summit 1.9 mi.
and points to the R, while the L fork crosses the stream and continues
through private land to the old Putnam Farm. Take the R fork.

The trail begins to climb moderately and then levels off at 1.1 mi.
and crosses a natural rock bridge over a rushing brook. A careful
check to the L and R of this reveals that the brook has carved a
tunnel-like cavern through the rock. Care should be exercised while
exploring, as the sides are steep and slippery.

After crossing the rock bridge the trail swings slightly R, and the
steeper climb up the ridge commences. At 1.2 mi. the trail begins to
be very steep, with numerous large boulders for the hiker to
negotiate.

The next 0.7 mi. of trail is very steep and zig-zags over and across
numerous ledges and large boulders. There are several lookouts with
wonderful views into the valley. Finally, at 1.7 mi. an exciting bare
rock area is encountered, offering more views to the SW. The trail is

unmarked here; but continue up the gently sloping wide rock face, and keep to the L. Cross the outlet of the pond to find the path and continue another 0.2 mi. to Crane Mt. Pond itself. The pond is dammed by beaver at the S end, which has raised the water level at least two feet.

To visit the NW ridge, which has no marked trail, turn L at the pond and begin a gentle climb in a general NNW direction. There are two or three faint herd paths that lead to several rocky outlooks on the ridge line to the L. It is an easy and pleasant bushwhack through attractive red pines for approximately 0.8 mi. to the bare rocks of the summit of the NW ridge of Crane Mt. Because there is not a marked trail, explorations will require a compass, although the hiker should have no difficulty as long as he or she continues up and not down! There are super views and exquisite scenery in this little-visited area.

To make a loop, return to the pond and continue the trip around it and up the main NW summit trail (see above).

Distances: To junction to Putnam Farm, 0.7 mi.; to Crane Mt. Pond, 1.9 mi.; to NW ridge rocks, 2.7 mi. (4.4 km.). Elevation of NW ridge, 2876 ft. (880 m.)

PROSPECT MT.

One of the most popular mountains in the state is Prospect Mt. Its summit can be achieved with minimal effort by almost everyone who drives up the Memorial Highway; but there is also an attractive foot trail that offers the hiker history and scenery although no views are available until the summit. (See ADK's *Guide to Adirondack Trails: Eastern Region* for another description of this trail.)

To reach the trailhead, turn W off NY9 onto Montcalm St. in the heart of Lake George village. Continue on Montcalm to its end where it intersects Cooper St. Here a sign directs hikers to the foot trail up a slight incline and through a tree-lined dirt path. However, there is little or no parking available, so it is suggested that the hiker turn R on Cooper St., go one block to West St. and turn L, then L again one additional block to Smith St. where plenty of parking spaces are to be found along the street and under the steps of the overpass that crosses the Northway.

The trail begins at the foot of the stairs and for the first 0.1 mi. crosses the Northway (I-87) on a modern, steel grid (see-through) bridge. Leaving the bridge, the trail begins to climb moderately. At 0.2 mi. it levels briefly and then jogs R at 0.25 mi.. At this point, and until it reaches and crosses the toll road at 0.5 mi., the trail uses the cobbled bed of the old cable railway that once carried Victorian families to the top of Prospect Mt. It is a steady, moderate climb. The path appears to be well used and is extremely easy to follow.

At the toll road, a sign warns the hiker not to walk on the road and points to the trail's continuation on the other side. On the opposite side of the road, the trail obviously leaves the railway bed. It continues to climb, gradually becoming steeper. A jog R occurs at 0.5 mi. where a L fork leads almost immediately into a clearing that perhaps once provided a view, now hidden by large trees and numerous shrubs. Here the footpath has been eroded to bedrock in many places, providing large stretches of bare rock to walk upon. The character of the forest is a mixture of various pines interspersed with groves of deciduous trees.

The path bends L at 0.8 mi. and continues climbing until at 0.9 mi. it briefly becomes very steep. A level area with pine needles underfoot is reached at 1.0 mi. After passing through this shaded and attractive area, the trail climbs again for a short stretch, coming to another fork at 1.2 mi. The R path leads one on with the promise of a lookout but, unfortunately, this one, too, has been long over-grown—although from the traffic the path gets, everyone seems to check it out.

Continuing L, the main trail climbs another short section until it reaches the toll road again at 1.3 mi. It crosses the road and proceeds to the R around a large rock outcropping, then turns L to enter the picnic area at the top. It reaches the true summit at 1.4 mi. on the opposite side of the picnic area, where the cab section of the old fire tower still stands on display.

Explore the civilized summit with the tourists who drove up. On the SE side are the remains of the cable gears for the old railroad. A sign says that the old cable railway was built in 1895 at a cost of $110,000 and operated for 8 years. It cost 50 cents to ride to the top. A rustic hotel, named the Prospect Mountain House, was built here in the 1870s and burned twice.

The views of Lake George and the surrounding mountains are wonderful on a clear day.

Distances: To first crossing of toll road, 0.5 mi.; to second crossing, 1.3 mi.; to summit, 1.4 mi. (2.3 km.). Elevation, 2041 ft. (622.3 m.); Ascent, 1600 ft. (489 m.).

Crane Mt. Firetower

WILCOX LAKE WILD FOREST AND BALDWIN SPRINGS SECTION

The Wilcox Lake Wild Forest and Baldwin Springs areas can be accessed by a number of trails and from several highways, including NY 30 and NY 8. The land is rugged, with a variety of terrain, including several small lakes and swamps. Although small wooded mountains dot the landscape, the only mountain worthy of climbing for its incredible views is Mt. Blue. Mt. Blue, however, is without a trail, and the shortest, most direct route requires a canoe or small boat to cross Garnet Lake to reach the trail that leads to the foot of the mountain where a bushwhack can begin.

The Wilcox Lake Wild Forest and Baldwin Springs section contains the most lengthy hikes in the southern region, and they are often muddy and difficult due to frequent use of many trails by ATVs and other off-road vehicles. Baldwin Springs, once the hub of several old roads which led into a tiny settlement and surrounding farms during the heyday of the lumber and tanning industries, is an attractive and interesting pine barrens. The spring that gives the clearing its name can still be found to the R of the trail register, welling up through the center of an ancient hollow log.

Recommended hikes in this section are:

MODERATE HIKES:

Round Pond from Garnet Lake—2.3 mi. A pleasant walk along a snowmobile trail to a seldom-visited little pond offering privacy and superb scenery.

Tenant Creek Falls—2.1 mi. Follow a woodland path upstream and visit three beautiful waterfalls.

HARDER HIKES:

Wilcox Lake from Brownell Camp—5.2 mi. A pleasant walk mostly along picturesque E. Stony Creek to the shores of attractive Wilcox Lake.

Mt. Blue—2.0 mi. (approx.) If you can obtain a small boat to cross the lake, bushwhack up this marvelous mountain for a super view you have to see to believe (on a clear day!).

TRAIL DESCRIBED	TOTAL MILES	PAGE
Round Pond via Mud Pond	1.7	47
Round Pond from Garnet Lake	2.3	49
Garnet Lake Canoe/Hike to Lizard		
Pond and Baldwin Springs	4.4	53
Baldwin Springs via W. Stony		
Creek Rd.	6.5	56
Indian Pond	1.0	57

Harrisburg Lake to Baldwin Springs		
via Arrow Trail	7.4	59
Tenant Creek Falls	2.1	62
Wilcox Lake from Brownell Camp		
via E. Stony Creek Trail	5.2	65
Wilcox Lake from Willis Lake	6.3	69

BUSHWHACK:

| Mt. Blue | 2.0 (approx.) | 51 |

ROUND POND VIA MUD POND

This is a short walk past an aptly named Mud Pond to a Round Pond that is really not round and is far prettier than its name suggests. The trail begins along a pleasant dirt road which leads to, and through, a private inholding that is currently posted against motor vehicles. Hikers may walk the marked DEC trail. A second, somewhat longer route to Round Pond is via the snowmobile trail that begins from the trailhead along the shore of Garnet Lake. (See below.)

Mud Pond is an extremely popular name for small bodies of water in the Adirondacks. Folklore has it that many attractive fishing lakes were so named by the old-time guides who thought people wouldn't be so likely to travel to them and spoil a good thing. This Mud Pond, however, is well on its way to becoming yet another swamp.

To reach the trailhead, drive W on Garnet Lake Road from the hamlet of Thurman. At 1.0 mi. past Little Pond, a small dirt road on the L (SW) is seen. It is marked with a brown and yellow DEC sign. If coming from the NE turn S off NY 8 onto Garnet Lake Road in the village of Johnsburg, and continue 2.0 mi. past the Garnet Lake turnoff. The DEC sign at the beginning of the small dirt road says

Mud Pond 0.6 mi. and Round Pond 1.6 mi. The hiker should park here on the shoulder of Garnet Lake Road, as the road marked as the trail is narrow and there are very few places to park along the 0.7-mi. length to the barrier prohibiting vehicles from invading private lands.

Begin walking on the smaller dirt road, which climbs gently through attractive open hardwoods before leveling off at 0.4 mi. The general direction is SW, and the road is well maintained and appears to receive little use. Although there are one or two places one could park along its shoulders, it is such a pleasant and short walk, why not burn more calories?

At 0.5 mi., after a short downhill section on the dirt road, a trail branches off to the L through a little clearing with numerous summer wildflowers. After a short 0.2 mi. descent the shore of Mud Pond is reached. There is a well-used camping area covered with lush grasses. And, indeed, this pond is aptly named as there is no approach to the water that does not require negotiating dark, muddy muck. Nevertheless it is an attractive little pond surrounded by water-loving plants that will help create a swamp in another 10 or 20 years.

Returning to, and then continuing along the dirt road, the hiker reaches a substantial iron barrier at 0.7 mi. that warns of "No Trespassing" to vehicles. A brown and yellow DEC trail sign merely warns the hiker that permission may have to be obtained to continue. The road/trail continues up a slight incline to a clearing at 0.9 mi. There is a brown cabin on the R and a private property sign tacked to a tree. Since the trail is still marked by DEC signs and no other posting, hikers should continue bearing L across the clearing in a generally SE (L) direction. Walk between a fat young spruce tree and an apple tree to find the continuation of the foot trail, which is marked with a sign prohibiting motorized vehicles except snowmobiles in winter. (If someone is in residence in the cabin, one should ask permission to continue.)

Entering the woods, the trail is well used and easy to follow. At

1.1 mi. it crosses a small stream and goes through a large berry patch; then enters the woods again at 1.2 mi. Here it is quite flat and very pleasant walking. Soon a descent begins, heading generally SE to Round Pond at 1.5 mi. The NE shore of Round Pond is reached at 1.7 mi. after the trail cuts through a small marshy area at the bottom of the hill.

To locate a tiny, sandy piece of shoreline, walk R about 250 yds. through the woods. Although there is no well-defined path, it is not difficult to find. Round Pond is at least three-quarters surrounded by swamplands, but it is still well worth the relatively short walk to enjoy this unusually pristine setting.

Distances: To Mud Pond, 0.7 mi.; to brown cabin, 0.9 mi.; to Round Pond, 1.7 mi. (2.7 km.).

ROUND POND FROM GARNET LAKE

There are two routes into this extremely pretty, little-visited pond. (See above for Round Pond via Mud Pond.) The most direct is to take the snowmobile trail that begins from the parking area on the E side of Garnet Lake. To reach Garnet Lake take Garnet Lake Road from Thurman if coming from the S, or if coming from NY 8 in the village of Johnsburg, turn S onto Garnet Lake Road. (The extension road leading to Garnet Lake itself is a SW turn off Garnet Lake Road, very near the place were the road becomes dirt instead of macadam.)

The parking area is 0.9 mi. from the L turn at the T near the dam end of the lake, just before a barrier that prohibits the public from driving through the private camps farther S on the lake. The parking area will hold 4 to 6 vehicles; in summer it is heavily used by fishermen and canoeists because a very small boat access area is opposite the parking area. The trail sign is difficult to spot among the foliage, but it points the way to Round Pond, indicating that the hike is 2.3 mi., which is accurate.

The trail begins on the L (N) side of the parking area. It immediately begins a brief ascent of the ridge as it parallels the road for a short distance. The trail is sporadically marked with orange snowmobile signs. The forest is mostly mixed hardwoods—beech, maple and birch with an occasional fragrant balsam.

A small wet area can be rock-hopped at 0.2 mi. The general direction is S, and the trail here is very level and pleasant walking. Another wet area occurs at 0.3 mi. Very soon after crossing it, a large collection of attractive mossy boulders is seen on the L, many 30 to 35 ft. high. The trail continues along a flat plateau and enters, at 0.4 mi., a handsome stand of hardwoods. Here it is even and easy going through the open woods.

Now begins a brief descent at 0.6 mi.; the general direction is S. The trail bends to the R past several enormous yellow birches at 0.7 mi. One tree is at least 8 ft. in circumference. At 0.8 mi. a faint path forks off to the R, but the main trail is marked with a sign pointing L. The trail bends slightly R and passes over several little undulations, beween which are tiny wet areas. The woods are still open as the trail parallels a stream for about 250 yds.; it then makes a slight bend to the L and begins to climb a long ridge.

A leveling off occurs at 1.0 mi. and the general direction is now SE. Steady climbing commences again as the trail becomes steeper at 1.2 mi. and reaches the height of land at 1.3 mi. It begins a bit of descent to cross a swift small stream at 1.4 mi., and then briefly turns R to parallel this stream for a short time. Then a gentle bend R occurs, signaling the beginning of the ascent of yet another ridge.

At 1.6 mi. a brief level area is traversed. The trail enters a rock-strewn area and proceeds through a dry gully, climbing again although moderately. At 1.8 mi. the descent to Round Pond begins, and at 2.3 mi. the shore of the pond is reached.

Although this W side of Round Pond is marshy and access to the water is marginal, one can bushwhack L (N) to reach higher land and a few possible camping areas. Although none appear to be used frequently, there is evidence of previous campfires.

Round Pond is very attractive with several rocky outcroppings and a wide variety of trees and colorful plants lining its shores.

Distances: To large boulders, 0.3 mi.; to height of land, 1.3 mi.; to Round Pond, 2.3 mi. (3.7 km.).

MT. BLUE

PARTIAL BUSHWHACK

Pristine and incredibly attractive, this relatively easy, trailless mountain rewards the adventurous bushwhacker with outstanding views from its many bare lookouts, and a summit of sublime pleasures. To reach the foot of the mountain, the hiker must either canoe across Garnet Lake or take the marked trail from the SW through Baldwin Springs to Lizard Pond and then to the end of Lizard Pond's marsh. (See below for Lizard Pond and Baldwin Springs trail description.)

The quickest and most scenic route to the trailhead to Lizard Pond and the cutoff point at the foot of Mt. Blue is to launch a canoe or other small boat, and paddle across Garnet Lake. (See above, Round Pond from Garnet Lake, for directions to Garnet Lake.) Small boats can be launched across from the parking turnout on Garnet Lake's shore road. Since Garnet Lake's shores are either privately owned or surrounded by swampland, it is not possible to walk around the lake to the trailhead from either direction.

After launching the canoe, paddle SW or directly across to the W shore, and then turn S (L) to follow the lake shore approximately 1.0 mi. to the trailhead, which is directly across from the tip of the E peninsula's point. Paddle close to the W shore to an obviously well-used, grassy clearing. There is a DEC trail sign indicating the trail to Lizard Pond a bit farther back from the shore, which cannot be readily seen. Leave the canoe or boat here in order to walk the trail to Lizard Pond and/or to bushwhack up Mt. Blue. There is no herd path up Mt. Blue, so a map and compass are a must, especially for the first part of the climb after one leaves the trail.

Marked for snowmobiles and hikers, the trail to Lizard Pond begins climbing almost immediately, and is rough and rocky underfoot. There is a brief level section at 0.2 mi., after which it continues to climb the ridge at a moderate incline with a slight bend to the R at 0.25 mi.

The forest is mixed evergreens and hardwoods, with several mature specimens intermingled, making an attractive, high and open canopy of greenery. At 0.3 mi. the trail crosses a very small brook, after which a wet area must be negotiated. Continuing to climb at 0.5 mi., the trail passes through a heavy understory of witch hobble. At 0.7 mi. the end of the Lizard Pond Vly is seen through the trees. Here, too, the trail levels off. The hiker who wishes to climb Mt. Blue should cut off to the N (R) and begin bushwhacking up the shoulder of a small knoll in order to begin the climb up Mt. Blue.

Two small knolls are traversed in the beginning, with quick descents into tiny valleys, before the climb up Mt. Blue begins in earnest. Consult the compass frequently, and travel in a general NNW direction. Hikers should watch the contours of the land, and stay to the high ground, traveling along the SE shoulder of the mountain.

At approximately 1.5 mi. the hiker begins to encounter bare rock stretches. Lookouts afford stunning views as more and more elevation is gained. Mt. Blue was burned by a devastating fire during the early 1900s and the bare rock slopes are a direct result. However, they do provide the hiker with outstanding vistas at many points, in addition to the summit.

The summit is reached at approximately 2.0 mi. Because it is relatively flat and contains extensive stretches of bare rock, there are several viewing locations. To the E and NE are the craggy cliffs of Crane Mt. and the jewel-like waters of Garnet Lake, and to the S is Lizard Pond, Bearpen Peak, Baldhead and Moose Mts. Hikers should spend time exploring to discover small cleared overlooks offering a magnificent variety of spectacular scenes—especially on a crisp, clear day.

Distances: To beginning of vly, 0.7 mi.; to summit of Mt. Blue, 2.0 mi. (3.2 km.). Ascent, 1400 ft.; Elevation, 2925 ft.

GARNET LAKE CANOE/HIKE TO
LIZARD POND AND BALDWIN SPRINGS

This trail is long and very attractive. It traverses mostly flat areas and goes through some beautiful and unusual old white pine groves enroute from Lizard Pond (sometimes spelled Lixard, thought to be a misspelling that remains on many maps) to Baldwin Springs. (See above, Round Pond from Garnet Lake, for directions to Garnet Lake shore parking area.)

A popular put-in point along Garnet Lake is located across from a small DEC parking area that accommodates 4 or 5 cars. Here one can park and begin the paddle up and across the lake. Canoe SW; the hiking trail begins on the W shore directly across from the narrowest section at the S end of the lake opposite the peninsula that juts out on the E shore.

The landing and take-out area at the trailhead is sandy, flat, and very pretty, a grassy clearing shaded by several large maples. It is large enough to store several canoes and still leave space for picnickers. A DEC trail sign says Lizard Pond 1.0 mi. This is correct, but if the lean-to is to be the destination, add another 0.5 mi. to include the trail around the marsh and pond.

The trail leads to the W away from the lake and immediately

begins a moderate uphill climb. At 0.2 mi. it levels briefly and at 0.3 mi., after a short dip, continues climbing. Yellow or red snowmobile signs occasionally mark the way. A wet area is encountered at 0.4 mi. and then the trail levels briefly, leading around or over a blowdown.

The trail continues to climb, making a tiny dip at 0.5 mi. where, on the L, is a small ravine. The top of the ridge is reached at 0.6 mi. This is also the beginning of the marsh that has gradually filled in the E end of Lizard Pond.

Jogging L, the trail rises about two ft., paralleling the edge of the marsh and continuing through a stand of hemlocks. The marsh can be seen intermittently through the trees. It deserves a closer look as it is a very interesting and beautiful area filled with a large variety of flowers in season and groves of young tamaracks.

Some small ups and downs are traversed until, at 0.9 mi., a side trail cuts R for 50 yds. to provide an unrestricted first view of the pond. Back on the main trail, a small brook is crossed at 1.0 mi. This is the outlet of the pond.

After a short rise and curve L, the trail turns away from the pond to climb a small ridge whose crest is reached at 1.1 mi., where the pond can be seen through the trees. After traversing an attractive grove of hemlock and paper birch, the trail reaches a lean-to at 1.3 mi. Relatively new, it sits on a small knoll overlooking the W end of the pond. The stark cliffs of Mt. Blue are seen directly across the pond, and the dramatic crags of Crane Mt. are seen in the distance looking NW.

To Baldwin Springs:

Continuing W to Baldwin Springs, at 1.4 mi. the trail is pleasant and well defined with occasional rocky and rough areas. The end of Lizard Pond is reached at 1.5 mi. The trail now turns L through a marshy area in a NW direction. The trail bends R at 1.7 mi. and spans a wet area on a primitive log corduroy that is extremely slippery when wet.

Descending slightly at 1.8 mi. through a mucky area, the trail turns SW and passes through a ravine. Here the trail, wildly overgrown with ferns and witch hobble, is difficult to discern.

Traversing the side of a small ridge, the trail is still hard to follow. At 1.9 mi. a bridge crosses a brook and then in another 10 yds. a second, spanking-new bridge (in 1987—with railings!) crosses another stream. The trail turns L and goes quite close to the bank of the stream for the next 0.3 mi., still traveling W.

At 2.0 mi., still paralleling the stream, the trail bends to the R through a level valley and once more is easy to follow. After a slight bend L the direction becomes more SW. The stream is crossed again at 2.1 mi. by rock-hopping. At 2.3 mi. another stream is crossed on yet another brand new wood-plank bridge.

A thicket of tall hemlocks entered at 2.5 mi. provides very pleasant and cool walking. The trail varies from easy to rough and wet, but the wetter sections have plenty of rocks on which to walk. At 2.8 mi. large white pines predominate. A larger wet area tests one's balance for approximately two-tenths of a mile, beginning at 3.1 mi. At 3.4 mi. a vly comes into view on the L. The trail ascends into a stand of scrubby spruce at 3.5 mi.

The trail reaches a junction at 3.7 mi. To the L is Indian Pond, actually a large marsh, and the trail leading to it is an overgrown snowmobile trail. (See below.) The sign says Indian Pond 0.8 mi.; Lizard Pond 2.4 mi; Garnet Lake 3.4 mi.; W Stony Creek Road 1.6 mi. These all appear to be short by 0.3 mi.

At 3.8 mi. another new snowmobile bridge spans a small stream. Watch for the showy purple fringed orchis which blooms here in June and July. The trail now enters a grove of hemlocks and very soon passes two enormous glacial erratics on the R.

The character of the trail begins to change as the sandy pine barrens of Baldwin Springs are approached. As the trail enters the scrubby pines and sedge grasses, there are also numerous sun-loving plants such as the beautiful orange hawkweed, wild strawberries, and, everywhere, blueberries. At 4.2 mi. the junction of the Fish Pond trail is reached. Continue L for another 0.2 mi. to cross the bridge over Stony Creek and into the main clearing of Baldwin Springs at 4.4 mi.

Distances: To end of Lizard Pond marsh, 0.6 mi.; to Lizard Pond lean-to, 1.3 mi.; to white pine forest, 2.8 mi.; to Indian Pond junction, 3.7 mi.; to Fish Ponds trail junction, 4.2 mi.; to Baldwin Springs, 4.4 mi. (7.1 km.).

BALDWIN SPRINGS VIA W. STONY CREEK ROAD

Baldwin Springs is an interesting, sprawling area of sand barrens with numerous clearings, interspersed with several species of pines. The place gets its name from a cool spring that wells up from the earth and is a possible source of drinking water. It can be located about 20 ft. to the R of the trail register, next to a hummock of shrubs. Look for a large hollow log set into the ground. The current prevalence of *giardia lambia* or ("beaver fever") should make the hiker cautious about any water source, so it is advised that all drinking water be carried in or boiled at least three minutes.

Baldwin Springs was one of several short-lived, tiny settlements that sprang up in response to farming and lumbering in the north country. Its current accessibility is limited to four-wheel-drive and ATV vehicles. It is a popular camping area; in winter, deer-watching is the local attraction for snowmobilers, as in recent years deer have yarded in the area.

This makes an interesting destination, or starting point, for the hiker since five trails begin or end here. Be advised that driving the road is **not recommended** for regular two-wheel-drive, low-slung vehicles. Although it is maintained through the summer months, several sections are subject to frequent flooding and wash-outs.

To reach Baldwin Springs by the road, drive from Stony Creek on Harrisburg Road, turn N (R) on Wolf Point Road and drive 0.9 mi. to an unsigned road on the L. This is W. Stony Creek Road. Turn here and continue W 6.5 mi. to the T intersection at Baldwin Springs. To the R (N) is a pine grove and fireplace with a picnic table that sees extensive use, while taking the L (S) along the road for another 0.7 mi. will bring one to the Dog and Pup Club, a private in-holding, although hiking across the land is permitted.

It is necessary to cross E. Stony Creek to reach the trail register and the spring. Vehicles must ford the shallow water, and can at several points. There are two bridges for the hiker. One crossing is possible on an iron catwalk W of the picnic grove. A second foot and snowmobile bridge is found by taking the L (S) branch of the T and going 0.2 mi. to a knoll and DEC trail sign which says Baldwin Springs 0.3 mi. to the R.

Explore the maze of vehicle trails tangled through the pines. The forests in this area are mainly used by the motorized set of campers and forest lovers. Hikers may find the mud and motors distracting. (For trail descriptions into the area, see trails above and below, where Baldwin Springs is the destination.)

Distances: Wolf Point Road to T intersection, 6.5 mi. (10.1 km.); to footbridge across E. Stony Creek, 6.7 mi. (10.8 km.); to Baldwin Springs trail register, 7.0 mi. (11.3 km.)

INDIAN POND

This hike is a short, beautiful walk through an old pine forest to the banks of a tiny pond on Madison Creek. At one time this shallow pond, created at the turn of the century by the damming of Madison Creek, was a mile or more in length. With the destruction of the dam, the area has returned to boggy swampland. The narrow, mile-long pond still shows on the topographic map but all that remains now is the memory. Occasionally beaver will enlarge sections of the swamp, recreating a pond for a few years, but recently (1987) the latest beaver dam was breached and the flow is once more narrow, meandering through wet marshlands. But the walk to the site of the old dam is very attractive and worthy of the effort, if only to enjoy the murmur of the ancient pine forest through which the trail passes.

The marked snowmobile trail into Indian Pond from Stony Creek Road is located two miles E of the Baldwin Springs junction (see above). The trail is well marked with snowmobile disks and a brown DEC trail sign prominently mounted near its beginning.

Parking along the shoulder of the dirt road is not recommended as here it is narrow and the shoulders soft and sandy, but a small cleared area about 50 yds. to the E on the N side is large enough for two or three vehicles.

As the trail begins, note the enormous white pine to the R. This is just the first of many ancient pines found growing in the forest traversed by this trail. At 0.1 mi. a second trail is encountered; the L (N) branch leads towards Indian Pond and the marshlands.

After a turn N (L) here, the trail very shortly crosses a plank snowmobile bridge that spans a tiny stream. Interrupted ferns, bunchberries, and many other lush green plants fight for growing space among the brown pine needles underfoot. The trail is soft and springy, flat and attractive, with occasional rocks to add interest.

At 0.5 mi. a small wet area is crossed, and a curve L occurs at 0.7 mi. On the L the marsh comes into sight. A great deal of beaver activity is evidenced on the L at 0.8 mi. by the many stripped and downed saplings. The shore of Indian Pond comes into view at 0.9 mi.

A large rock, right at the end of the trail and partially underwater, may offer a place to sit and enjoy a picnic, if the water level isn't too high. The tiny pond is hardly worthy of the name at present, and the remains of the man-made dam are buried in a broken beaver dam.

Although it is possible to continue to the W of the pond and cross to the other side on the beaver dam, the continuation of this snowmobile trail to Lizard Pond is not passable for the hiker, as it traverses swamplands in several sections.

Distances: To snowmobile bridge, 0.1 mi.; to beaver site, 0.7 mi.; to Indian Pond, 1.0 mi. (1.6 km.).

HARRISBURG LAKE TO BALDWIN SPRINGS VIA ARROW TRAIL

The Arrow Trail is long and arduous, made more so by the location of the trailhead, which requires walking an extra 3.0 mi. on a very badly rutted and muddy dirt road unsuitable for normal vehicular use. To the N the Baldwin Springs entrance is equally difficult to reach, since the 6.5-mi. road to the Springs is extremely rough and subject to wash-outs with every rainstorm. (See above.) This would, however, make a challenging backpacking trip.

To reach the Arrow trailhead to Baldwin Springs, take Harrisburg Road W out of Stony Creek and pass through Knowelhurst, then on to Harrisburg, which is a hamlet of summer homes. There is a parking area on the R just before Harrisburg Lake. Here is a trail register; brown and yellow DEC signs point to the blue-marked trail which is a continuation of the road, now changed to dirt. A walk from here to the beginning of the trail into the forest is approximately 3.0 mi. over this woods road, passable only to four-wheel-drive vehicles or ATVs.

The road traverses several steep ridges and is a challenge in itself. It is, however, another possible walking route to Wilcox Lake, too. (See above.) On dry summer or fall days the courageous hiker may be able to drive across the old wooden bridge and on the dirt road for approximately 2.0 mi. to park at the top of a rise in a cleared area where the old Arrow Trail began.

The Arrow Trail originally started from this clearing at the top of the big ridge about 1.0 mi. E of the current state trailhead. This cleared section once served as a roundout area where the logs were gathered and loaded for the trip out of the woods. For many years an old wagon axle marked with a big arrow stood in the clearing, pointing the way to the trail. The axle has rusted away, although signs of the original trail are still in evidence here. The land is now privately owned, so the hiker must travel an additional mile to state lands and the newer "Arrow Trail." Parking is available only at the side of the road.

The trail begins on the R at the bottom of a dip in the road approximately 1.0 mi. from the clearing described above. A DEC sign says Baldwin Springs 7.5 mi. via the Arrow Trail. (This mileage is correct to the trail register at Baldwin Springs.) It begins by heading E and slightly uphill. The trail is in good condition, with a few wet areas, and for the next mile goes gradually uphill. At 1.1 mi. it bends L and then continues steeply uphill to the top of a ridge at 1.3 mi. The trail then descends to join an orange-marked snowmobile trail at 1.4 mi. Turn R, although there is no trail sign here. The L leads to a swamp and E. Stony Creek, passable only when frozen by the cold of winter.

Turning R, the trail becomes rocky and wet for the next tenth of a mile and then begins to climb moderately. The forest is open mature hardwoods: yellow birch, maple and beech trees with occasional clumps of dark green hemlocks. At 1.7 mi. the trail passes through a grove of attractive, mature hemlocks. It then crosses a small brook which has no bridge at 1.9 mi., and continues uphill and swings slightly to the R. The top of a ridge is reached at 2.0 mi. and the trail bears to the R again. The trail is mostly flat at this point, the general direction being NNE.

At 2.4 mi. is an intersection with the old road, which is rutted and torn by the passage of ATVs. The R turn leads along the original Arrow Trail back through private land. Take the L turn to continue toward Baldwin Springs.

The trail reaches a brook at 2.7 mi. and is now rocky, wet and downhill. It crosses another creek at 2.9 mi. and a flat area after climbing another small ridge. At 3.4 mi. there is a benchmark on the rock to the R at the top of a knoll, next to an enormous hemlock tree. The trail crosses a larger stream at 3.5 mi. The woods are lush and open. It begins climbing away from the stream bed and at 3.3 mi. crosses another small stream. At 3.9 mi. the large wooden bridge over Hill Creek, one of the major tributaries of E. Stony Creek, is reached.

After crossing the bridge the trail makes a sharp R and then heads L to begin to ascend a ridge. It is wide and easy walking along the old road through young hardwoods, probably lumbered within the last 10 or 15 years. Now the trail goes up a ridge and levels off at 4.6 mi. At 5.0 mi. a branch L leads to a beaver dam. Between 6.0 mi. and 6.1 mi., four wet areas are encountered in quick succession. The trail shows evidence of frequent use by off-road vehicles.

At 6.4 mi. the trail is overgrown and brushy, but very easy to follow due to its width. Now the pine barrens and open areas of Baldwin Springs begin to be encountered as the trail approaches Madison Creek. Paper birch, balsam and spruce are abundant. At 6.5 mi. a fork R leads from the main trail to the rickety footbridge across Madison Creek. (If you continue another 150 ft. on the main trail, you will have to wade the fording area.) After the trail crosses this swift-running section, the private in-holding of the Dog and Pup Club is crossed. Continuing past the clubhouse to the main road, at 7.1 mi. the trail reaches the cutoff to the footbridge and the hub of Baldwin Springs. The trail turns L here to cross the bridge, then continues until at 7.3 mi. it turns L at the next intersection to reach the trail register at 7.4 mi. (See above, Baldwin Springs via W. Stony Creek Rd.)

Distances: Trailhead to snowmobile trail, 1.4 mi.; to junction of original Arrow Trail, 2.4 mi.; to Hill Creek bridge, 3.9 mi.; to Madison Creek bridge, 6.5 mi.; to cutoff and bridge to Baldwin Springs, 7.1 mi.; to Baldwin Springs trail register, 7.4 mi. (12.0 km.).

TENANT CREEK FALLS

Three lovely waterfalls are the reward for this short walk which, in the beginning, follows an old overgrown logging road but then becomes a semi-bushwhack, traversing a faint footpath upstream. The hiker will have to cross Tenant Creek, which may provide a bit of a challenge in the spring and other times of high water.

For directions on how to reach the trailhead at Brownell Camp, see Wilcox Lake from Brownell's Camp, below. Park in the clearing on the L and take the trail that leads N along E. Stony Creek. The land to the R is the old Brownell Lumber Camp, which has been privately owned for many years. The present owners do not want hikers walking past their buildings, and they ask that you grant them privacy by taking the trail 0.3 mi. and then crossing Tenant Creek on the DEC snowmobile bridge.

Immediately after crossing the bridge, take the footpath E (R). This path shortly fades since many different places are used by hikers to recross Tenant Creek, and it appears there is no "best place" at present. Therefore, travel along the creek on this N side for approximately 0.1 to 0.2 mi. and choose a shallow section to cross. In summer or fall this will not be difficult as there are numerous rocks one can use. At certain times during high water in the spring, this crossing may not be possible.

After crossing the creek, climb the small ridge on the other side and there find a well-worn footpath which is an old logging road, leading upstream on the S side of Tenant Creek. Here the path is well defined although unmarked and unmaintained. At approximately 0.7 mi. it traverses a swampy area, and then rises again above the creek. This section is through an open hardwood forest and is very pleasant to walk.

After the trail crosses a tiny creek, an open knoll dotted with several mature evergreens is seen on the R. Then, continuing down a dip in the trail, the first of the three picturesque waterfalls appears at 0.9 mi. The waters are crystal clear and large rocks form a small natural amphitheater that invites a stop for rest and exploration.

The path continues up the ridge above the falls and is shaded by large hemlocks. Gradually, however, it becomes rougher and harder to follow, but if, occasionally, it is lost, the hiker need only continue to follow the creek on the L. At 1.2 mi. there are several enormous yellow birches that were spared during the last lumbering of this section.

At 1.3 mi. the path crosses a second small creek and veers briefly away from Tenant Creek to avoid a large marshy area. The easy footpath has now become a small rocky trail. At 1.8 mi. a large hemlock-covered ridge rises to the R. After climbing this, the faint foot trail descends the ridge and continues along the creek again.

At 2.0 mi. the second waterfall is reached. The third waterfall is another 250 yds. upstream. Each is uniquely attractive, and although small (30 to 50 ft.) as waterfalls are measured, the wild, scenic glen is filled with beauty and appears to be seldom visited.

There is a second route to the falls, but access must be gained by crossing private land. However, an interesting loop hike can be made by using this route on the return. The loop route utilizes an old, long abandoned road built by the CCC during the Depression. Its access point from the paved portion of E. Stony Creek Road is on the L, 200 yds. up a private driveway, 2.0 mi. from the trailhead at Brownell's (or 5.4 mi. from the turn onto E. Stony Creek Road from Old Northville Road). The owner of the beginning of this driveway, which is marked by a large ''Private'' sign hanging on a chain across the entrance (1987), asks that hikers take care not to block the road, and to use care not to infringe on the privacy of the two camps 0.4 mi. beyond.

To make a return loop, the hiker can reach the old CCC road from the third waterfall using a herd path heading R away from the stream and up the steep ridge. In 0.2 mi., at the top of this ridge, the level roadbed will be found with no difficulty. Turn S and continue following the road downhill for another 1.9 mi. back to E. Stony Creek Road.

The old road shows prominently on the topographic map but is now almost exclusively on private land. The present owner of the S end advised this writer that he does not object to hikers as long as they respect the privacy of the camps and homes in the area. The N section of the CCC road above the third waterfall is, however, firmly posted against trespassing. A turn L (N) when one reaches the old road will lead 0.2 mi. to the posted turnaround, located on an attractive knoll.

It is a delightful trek to walk the flat road through mature forests, as it follows the ridge line in a straightforward manner. Upon reaching E. Stony Creek Road again, hikers who have not spotted a car will need to walk the 2.0 mi. back to the Brownell Camp parking area.

Distances: To first waterfall, 0.9 mi.; to second waterfall, 2.0 mi.; to third waterfall, 2.05 mi. (3.1 km.). To make a loop trip, 6.0 mi. (9.6 km.).

WILCOX LAKE FROM BROWNELL CAMP
VIA E. STONY CREEK TRAIL

Wilcox Lake is one of the most attractive bodies of water in the southern Adirondacks and also one of the most popular. Overused but much appreciated, this small lake is a worthwhile destination for the day hiker.

The walk to Wilcox Lake from Brownell Camp along the E. Stony Creek Trail is very attractive yet only moderately strenuous. It traverses, for the most part, an old road through an open forest of mixed hardwoods and evergreens. This hike is recommended for those who enjoy walking more level areas, as the uphill sections are invigorating, but not difficult. Walking along the banks of picturesque E. Stony Creek for three-quarters of the way displays the lowlands of the southern Adirondacks at their best. Furthermore, Wilcox Lake is a worthy destination, despite sections of trail erosion, especially in the last mile (1985), by illegal dirt bikes and ATVs.

To reach the trailhead at Brownell Camp, take NY 30 (S to N) and, after crossing the bridge that spans E Stony Creek N of Great Sacandaga Lake, drive another 0.5 mi. and turn R onto Old Northville Road. Continue another 1.5 mi. and turn L at E. Stony Creek Road where a brown and yellow sign declares this to be the Town of Hope. Proceed for 7.4 mi. on this winding road, which has no signs proclaiming its name, almost to the end. The road is dirt for the last 1.5 mi. A parking area on the L has space for five or six vehicles, right before the entrance to the old lumber camp known as Brownell's. No Trespassing signs are prominently posted here, and although the present owners still permit access to this beautiful area, they request that hikers respect their privacy and walk the marked trail.

Brown and yellow DEC signs point to the trail, which begins to the R, going N, and follows the banks of E. Stony Creek. A trail register is on the R, approximately 50 yds. from the trailhead. Although the land is posted against everything except hiking, skiing and snowmobiles, there is evidence of repeated use as a camping area for the first 0.2 mi. At 0.2 mi. a fairly new wood-plank snowmobile bridge spans Tenant Creek, just before it rushes into E. Stony. The bridge is built high above the water, with sturdy handrails and enormous support logs (no doubt because the previous bridge, also new at the time, was washed out during the spring runoff a few years ago). Crossing this bridge, the trail proceeds straight ahead through a stand of white pine. An unmarked trail that turns R immediately after the bridge is the beginning of the herd path to Tenant Creek Falls. (See above.)

At 0.4 mi. a gentle climb begins and the trail bends R away from the creek. The climb avoids wet areas and takes the hiker part way up the shoulder of the small unnamed mountain on the L. The trail is well marked by blue DEC trail markers as well as shiny, bright-orange snowmobile disks, and occasional faded yellow ones.

At 0.6 mi. the first of several corduroys and boardwalks spanning wet areas is encountered, but soon the trail becomes pleasantly flat and free of debris and blowdown, due in part to illegal use by ATV riders. In this section the forest is quite open, composed of mixed hardwoods with a scattering of hemlocks. The trail traverses the contour of a ridge in a gentle series of ups and downs and at 0.7 mi. finally levels off.

At 1.0 mi., the descent of the ridge commences. A second small, wooden boardwalk is reached at 1.1 mi. and a rougher trail section at 1.2 mi. Two additional small wooden bridges cross wet areas at 1.3 mi. and then the trail drops gently and enters a swampy clearing. Directly ahead is E. Stony Creek again, which the trail now parallels for most of the next three miles. There is a fisherman's path off to the L, but the main trail crosses a muddy inlet (no bridge) and turns R (NE) in the upstream direction.

This is a very attractive section. The boulder-strewn creek displays a variety of flowers along its banks during the warm seasons. Pink Joe Pye weed and bright red cardinal flowers, among others, can be found in riotous profusion in midsummer.

The trail passes through a hemlock grove at 1.5 mi., turns briefly R, and then at 1.6 mi. returns quite close to the creek bank. It becomes wet and rocky at 1.7 mi., then rises slightly, and at 2.0 mi. begins to pull away from the stream again. The trail crosses a large inlet at 2.1 mi., turns R briefly, climbs a short incline and becomes level again along the bank.

Once more, at 2.7 mi., after a gentle series of ups and downs, the trail bears R (E) and up. At 2.9 mi. a larger wet area is encountered, but paths lead around it to the R and L. A large blowdown of four to five large pines occurs at 3.0 mi. but the trail itself has been cleared. The stream can occasionally be seen and heard on the L as the trail continues up, climbing a ridge and passing through majestic hemlocks. At 3.1 mi. it reaches the crest of the ridge.

For a short time the trail is flat and easy to walk. Descending the ridge, it encounters another mucky spot at 3.2 mi. and turns R and crosses a brook at 3.3 mi. After a moderate up-and-down section another small stream is crossed at 3.4 mi. At 3.6 mi. the trail descends to a lovely clearing where an attractive wooden bridge spans Dayton Creek just before it flows into E. Stony.

The trail now becomes rougher, with areas of blowdown and rocky, wet sections at 3.8 mi. Next comes an "S" turn. At 4.0 mi. another swampy area and tiny pond are negotiated to the L. Finally, the Bakertown Bridge, which crosses E. Stony Creek, is reached at 4.2 mi. (The sign at this junction says it is 3.4 mi. back to Brownell's Camp, but this is incorrect, for the hiker will actually walk approximately 0.8 mi. farther.) Bakertown Bridge is a suspension bridge barely wide enough to accommodate a snowmobile and will, unfortunately, also accommodate illegal ATVs, permitting them another access route into this area.

After crossing the bridge, the trail swings slightly L and almost immediately begins climbing the ridge, gradually circling around and up. It flattens out briefly at 4.7 mi., going through an attractive stand of mature hardwoods consisting mostly of ash, beech, and birch.

At 4.9 mi. the top of the ridge and a trail junction are reached. According to the sign, Bakertown Bridge was 0.5 mi. It is actually 0.7 mi. Willis Lake is to the W 4.5 mi. (See below.) The third sign declares Wilcox Lake to be to the R and another 0.2 mi.

Turning R, the trail joins the jeep road from Harrisburg Lake at 5.0 mi. Here another DEC sign directs the hiker L along the road, which officially ends before the short descent to the lake. Although "Motorized Vehicles Prohibited" signs are posted and a barrier periodically replaced, the "trail" down to the lakeshore is used repeatedly and illegally by four-wheel-drive vehicles and ATVs which legally come in on the jeep trail. The jeep trail ends at the barrier. There is a 75-ft. wide eroded mud track leading down to the lakeshore and the lean-to.

Despite this, Wilcox Lake itself remains one of the prettiest jewels in the southern Adirondacks. Decorated with numerous large rocks along its shores and a handsome island with picturesque pines, it often rings with the cry of the loon. There are several camping areas along its S shore, and a second lean-to is reached by walking an additional 0.6 mi. along the shore to the L.

Distances: To E. Stony Creek, 1.3 mi.; to Dayton Creek, 3.6 mi.; to Bakertown Suspension Bridge, 4.2 mi.; to jeep road from Harrisburg Lake, 5.0 mi.; to Wilcox Lake shore, 5.2 mi. (8.4 km.).

WILCOX LAKE FROM WILLIS LAKE

A second approach to Wilcox Lake, in addition to the one from Brownell Camp (see above), can be made from the SE via the Willis Lake trail. This trail traverses rugged terrain in sections, traveling through some of the wildest areas of the Wilcox Lake Wild Forest.

To reach the trailhead drive N on NY 30 along the Sacandaga River and turn R onto Pumpkin Hollow Road, which is 0.3 mi. after a sign that says Town of Wells, near an establishment called the Alpine Inn. Continue driving on Pumpkin Hollow Road for 1.6 mi.— mostly uphill—until the DEC trail guideboards are seen on the L. Parking is available for several vehicles on both sides of the road, although in spring the shoulders are extremely soft.

Although it is sometimes possible to drive a regular vehicle on the unpaved road, which continues past Willis Lake for another mile, it is suggested that hikers leave their cars at the parking turnout on Pumpkin Hollow Road where on the E side the trail to Murphy Lake begins and on the W the trail to Pine Orchard. Hikers who elect to drive the additional mile may find the dirt road section impassable in spring and summer due to floods and washouts. There are few turnaround places and very limited parking where the iron DEC barrier is reached at the trailhead.

The road becomes a dirt road and climbs a long, gentle grade after leaving Willis Lake and the camps along its shore. It is very pleasant to walk, and passes a hunting camp on the left at 0.9 mi. It reaches a DEC iron barrier at 1.0 mi. Although there is a small grassy clearing, it provides sufficient parking for only one or two vehicles.

Almost immediately after the barrier, the trail crosses a small stream on a sturdy plank snowmobile bridge. It begins climbing a long ridge, passing through mixed hardwoods and evergreens. This is a continuation of the road that once led all the way through to Harrisburg Lake. It is fairly easy walking at this point. At 1.4 mi. the trail levels off and soon begins climbing through a washed-out, rocky and difficult section. The top of the ridge is reached at 1.6 mi., after which the trail quickly jogs R and then L. Here the trail passes through a stand of very large, old white pines.

A fork in the trail occurs at 1.7 mi. Either branch may be chosen, as they rejoin in another 0.5 mi., although the L one has a red trailmarker. The general direction is E. The trail now makes a few snake-like turns, and at 1.9 mi. begins to descend. Here it becomes rougher underfoot and wildly overgrown, but still discernible.

At 2.1 mi. a slight jog to the R occurs. The surrounding forest is still predominantly hardwoods with hemlocks and large white pines randomly encountered. There are also some very large maple trees that measure at least 4 ft. in circumference, obviously an area that escaped the most recent logging.

At 2.2 mi. a steep downhill section begins. At the bottom of this ridge is a brook, after which the trail bears L briefly. At 2.5 mi. there is a wet area, and then the trail bends L slightly.

A very pretty but small clearing, surrounded by hemlocks, is passed at 2.6 mi. Another small stream must be crossed at 2.7 mi., and then the trail makes a series of twists and turns until at 3.1 mi. it levels off again, passing through a valley containing a heavy stand of hemlocks.

The trail makes a series of rollercoaster ups and downs across a ridge until reaching and crossing a brook at 3.5 mi. A swift-running, small stream is encountered at 3.6 mi. and a swamp can be seen on the R. The trail now passes through very wild and little-used country traveling ENE through a ravine, twisting L and R through mostly flat terrain. At 4.3 mi. it reaches an unusually old grove of hemlocks, with trees measuring 6 to 8 ft. in circumference.

At 4.8 mi. a possible major problem is encountered—Wilcox Lake Outlet—a large, fast-running stream with no bridge at this writing (1986). The snowmobile bridge was washed out several years ago and has not been replaced. In the spring during high water, and in winter, it may not be feasible to continue.

In times of normal water levels, the hiker can cross on the rocks. After the crossing, the trail goes L along the outlet for about 60 yds., then bears R and continues up a ridge, climbing moderately to reach the top at 5.0 mi. Here an enormous white pine stands majestically at the side of the trail. The trail begins to descend, and at 5.1 mi. reaches a dry watercourse, then a small stream at 5.3 mi. The trail flattens out and turns R to climb another ridge in a SE direction.

Now the forest becomes lush and overgrown with small beech saplings. Many of the larger beech trees have died, but smaller ones are growing in great numbers. An impressive pine, with a trunk of more than 7 ft. in circumference, lies across the trail at 5.7 mi. At 5.8 mi. the trail descends through a very open and attractive beech, ash and maple forest.

Finally, a junction with the E. Stony Creek trail is reached at 6.1 mi. A guideboard says that Willis Lake is 4.5 mi., but this is short by 1.7 mi. Take the L fork to Wilcox Lake; the sign says 0.2 mi. farther, which is correct. Lovely Wilcox Lake is reached at 6.3 mi. (See above description, Wilcox Lake from Brownell Camp via E. Stony Creek Trail.)

Distances: To fork, 1.7 mi.; to Wilcox Lake Outlet, 4.8 mi.; to junction of E. Stony Creek Trail, 6.1 mi.; to Wilcox Lake shore, 6.3 mi. (10.1 km.).

Tenant Creek Falls

BENSON, WELLS AND SILVER LAKE WILDERNESS SECTION

Adventures both in history and the natural world await the hiker who explores this most attractive section of the southern Adirondacks. Accessed by N-S NY 30 and E-W NY 8 and drained by the various tributaries of the Sacandaga River and E. Stony Creek, it is decorated with lovely lakes and impassable swamps and vlys. The hiker will find terrain to suit every mood, although there is only one mountain with a trail to a bare summit—Cathead.

During the latter part of the last century, this area was settled by hearty, hard-working farmers, mill owners, lumbermen and tannery workers. The lumbermen stripped the land of its forests, depleting the resource responsible for their employment, while the farmers were slowly defeated by a harsh climate and stony soil. Chemical tanning processes soon negated the need for hemlock bark, and the lands and tiny towns were gradually abandoned. The forests slowly returned, and the overgrown roads to the old farms, mills and settlements are today's hiking and snowmobile trails.

The Silver Lake Wilderness Area is the only classified wilderness in the southern region. It is to be used without noticeable human intrusions, and access by motorized equipment is strictly prohibited. The Silver Lake Wilderness is named for a sparkling lake located in its interior, which is accessible to hikers using the Northville-Placid Trail (see N-P Trail below).

Because of the diverse but generally rolling terrain, cross-country skiing and snowshoeing are recommended for the trails in this section, although great care should be taken in winter when crossing some of the swift-running streams that have no bridges.

Hikes recommended in this section are:

SHORT HIKES:

Cathead Mt.—1.6 mi. A steep but short trek up a wonderful small mountain with a bald summit, manned fire tower and panoramic views.

Whitehouse to Big Eddy—2.0 mi. Walk an old road and cross a swift-running, shallow stream to get to the quiet waters of the W. Branch of the Sacandaga.

MODERATE HIKES:

Murphy Lake from Pumpkin Hollow Road—4.5 mi. A vigorous walk through attractive woods to the shores of a picturesque lake with enormous boulders along its shores.

Pine Orchard and Jimmy Creek—4.8 mi. Visit the site of one of the last stands of virgin white pines in the E.

HARDER HIKES:

Bartman Trail to Baldwin Springs—6.3 mi. Enroute, visit three ponds and travel along an ancient wagon road, now a trail that provides easy walking, although a round-trip is only for long-distance hikers.

Piseco to Upper Benson on the Northville-Placid Trail—23.1 mi. An excellent backpacking trail that provides plenty to see on a three-day, two-night trip.

KIBBY POND

Kibby Pond is a short hike up a long ridge (a climb of 600 ft.) and then down to the shores of a lovely little pond that is a favorite with trout fishermen. There are at least three camping areas with fire rings and relatively level tent sites.

The trailhead is on the S side of NY 8, 5.1 mi. W of the post office in Bakers Mills. A brown and yellow DEC sign is very obvious at the side of the road, which says Kibby Pond 1.8 mi. (It's actually 0.1 mi. more.) There is parking for two cars in the turnaround road at the beginning of the trail, but it is better to park on NY 8 as there is ample space on the flat, dry road shoulders to accommodate several cars.

The trail begins behind the hemlocks and immediately descends to cross a medium-sized stream which shortly will join the East Branch of the Sacandaga River. In spring and times of high water, this stream may present a problem for the hiker as there is no bridge. Flat exposed rocks normally form a series of stepping stones to the opposite side.

After crossing the stream, the trail begins an immediate ascent heading S and up a moderately steep grade that is very rocky and rough underfoot. Hemlocks predominate, with several mature maple trees. The trail snakes to the L and R several times as it ascends the ridge, picking the easiest way through the rock-strewn hillside. At 0.2 mi. the trail still climbs moderately; the direction is more SSE. The trail leaves the rocky areas behind and enters a mature hardwood forest with numerous wildflowers. Canadian lilies carpet the ground, with mosses and ferns in abundance. The trail now becomes level and very easy to walk.

A mucky area is encountered at 0.3 mi. Traverse it to the R or L. At 0.5 mi. the trail crosses a creek. Green mossy rocks along its banks create a very attractive section. The trail becomes steeper and at 0.8 mi. turns L through a wet area and then R again. Still climbing, it curves R. The forest here is open although the underbrush is more dense, and at 0.9 mi. a short descent occurs.

The trail crosses a tiny brook at 1.0 mi. and continues to meander R and L as it picks a way up the ridge. It begins to climb more steeply after crossing a wet area at 1.1 mi. At 1.2 mi. the trail still climbs and continues its switchbacking from R to L to moderate the pitch for the hiker. After a short level section a steep descent begins at 1.3 mi. and the trail hugs the contours of the small mountain to the N (L). At 1.6 mi. it flattens out again on the plateau. Beautiful rock formations can be seen to the L and up the hillside.

Kibby Pond is sighted through the trees at 1.8 mi. After a short but steep drop, the shore of this lovely little pond is reached at 1.9 mi.

Distances: To top of large ridge, 1.2 mi.; to Kibby Pond, 1.9 mi. (3.1 km.).

BARTMAN TRAIL VIA FISH PONDS
TO BALDWIN SPRINGS

This is an interesting and challenging hike along one of the many old routes to Baldwin Springs from the S. The trail is an old road that passes two pretty ponds—now well on their way to becoming bogs— and it is surprisingly flat, dry and easy going for the hiker.

To reach the trailhead proceed SW from Baker's Mills post office 1.1 mi. to Bartman Road on NY 8 . Turn L (S) onto Bartman Road. A DEC sign here indicates that the Bartman trailhead is in this direction. Drive 1.1 mi. to a T intersection, and turn R for another 2.7 mi. to the trailhead. The road may be rough and washed out, especially in spring, but a state parking area at 2.0 mi. can be used if it is necessary to walk the last 0.5 mi.

Assuming one can drive the last section of the road, park on the side of the road, near an old shed on the R. The road now quickly becomes very rough and rutted due to recent lumbering in the immediate area. There has been an extensive clearcutting of the trees on the private land just before the trail, leaving ugly slash and only a few scrubby saplings.

Walk along the road for 0.1 mi. to the trail sign and turn R onto a wide, grassy roadway, obviously an unused old road. It soon bends R and passes through an overgrown apple orchard and past the cellar foundations of an old farmhouse on the R. A stream must be crossed right after the old farm clearing; it has been widened by constant use as a fording spot but can be crossed carefully on several strategically placed rocks on the L side.

At 0.3 mi. the general direction is S and the old road passes through low scrubby thickets of hemlock and other young trees and shrubs, obviously an old field rapidly returning to a mature forest state. At 0.4 mi. the route bends R through a mucky area and a draw, crisscrossing from one side to the other. The forest is now more open, but the young hardwood trees are not large, indicating lumbering within the past 20 years.

At 0.5 mi. the trail crosses a rocky and flat area with some wet spots. A descent and bend to the L begins at 0.6 mi. The trail is very rocky, rough and washed out—still heading down at 0.8 mi., bearing L. It follows a tiny stream on the R, attractively decorated with mosses and small rocks, and soon crosses it.

At 0.9 mi. the trail continues to descend moderately through the draw and recrosses the creek. Continuing down the draw, it reaches the bottom at 1.1 mi. after passing through a beautiful stand of young balsam trees. A log bridge is used to cross the small stream again, and at 1.2 mi. a substantial snowmobile bridge crosses one of the major inlets to Fish Ponds. After crossing the inlet and curving L, the trail begins to climb moderately, then levels off and follows the contours and the ridge around the ponds, avoiding the swampy shoreline.

The first Fish Pond comes into view at 1.3 mi. The partial views of the pond from various sections of the ridge indicate that the pond is very pretty, although it is located in the center of a large swamp.

There appears to be only one camping spot, with reasonable access to the water, at 1.5 mi. It is, however, worth the walk to the pond to enjoy the quiet beauty.

The trail in this section is even and fairly easy walking, undulating on occasion and crossing small inlets from time to time. The general direction is W as the trail hugs the ridge along the pond. Shortly, however, it turns S again.

At 1.8 mi. the trail approaches a creek that has recently changed its course due to heavy flooding. The continuation of the old road can be discerned straight across the brook approximately 50 yds. (even though the snowmobile markers show a route to the W (R) to avoid the swift, but shallow stream directly ahead). The hiker can cross with no difficulty.

At 2.0 mi. a large mucky spot is passed on the L, and another again at 2.3 mi. The beautiful cinnamon fern can be seen in this wet area. The second Fish Pond is seen at 2.5 mi., and the trail continues along the old roadbed several ft. above the very wet and swampy shoreline. The pond is rapidly returning to marshland, although beaver have flooded a significant section recently, creating a pond once more.

At 3.1 mi. the trail reaches the junction of the snowmobile trail to North Bend. The old road continues to the S (L fork). (The SW fork leads immediately into a swampy section for approximately one-half mile.) Continue on the old road and cross a tiny brook. At 3.2 mi. a larger brook flows with vigor through large moss-covered rocks, which the hiker has no trouble hopping across.

A sharp division occurs in the forest composition at 4.0 mi. immediately after the trail crosses a medium-sized creek. Here the hardwoods end abruptly and the trail enters a large stand of good-sized hemlocks. The sharp-eyed hiker may find evidence of bear, coyote and deer.

Soon the trail enters a ravine between two small mountains. It criss-crosses from one side to the other several times, seeking the best passage. Although the old roadbed appears at times to have been scarred badly by rampaging waters, by and large it is still very flat and dry and easy to walk. At 4.8 mi., the trail leaves the ravine and hugs the ridge on the W (R) going in a S direction.

At 5.1 mi. it leads through a rocky, wet and mucky area and then across a small stream. There is a clearing at 5.2 mi., and here the evidence of wheeled vehicles begins. The trail becomes increasingly rutted and muddy, until at 5.8 mi. a junction is reached. Brown and yellow DEC signs point the way to Baldwin Springs and Indian Pond straight ahead (no mileage given) and NE to Lizard Pond 3.1 mi. and Garnet Lake 4.1 mi.

Continuing straight for another 0.5 mi. to Baldwin Springs, the trail crosses a large stream on a sturdy plank snowmobile bridge and ends in the large grassy clearing of Baldwin Springs. Here there is a trail register and several campsites scattered among the pines and maze of dirt trails.

An old spring can still be found to the R of the trail register. It is partially hidden in the grasses in front of a clump of shrubs. Long ago an ancient upended hollow log was set into the spring, creating a small log well. Since there are a few resident frogs, and probably other water creatures living in the log, it is best to get spring water to the L, down the incline, where it runs out of the hillside. The water then runs through a small grassy depression and into a mud hole. This area was dammed by beaver several years ago, but recently it has been used by four-wheel-drive vehicles as a mud arena.

A loop trip from Baldwin Springs to North Bend and back to Fish Ponds is possible using the snowmobile trail that begins from the pine-ringed clearing known as North Bend. This trail, which runs NE along the Fish Ponds swamp extension, is not recommended to the hiker. The 4.2 mi. to the junction of the Fish Ponds trail is overgrown and difficult to follow. The snowmobile disks are spaced too far apart and cannot be depended upon to mark the way. Moreover, the trail is extremely rough, with numerous slippery rocks hidden in the leaves and undergrowth, and swampy and boggy areas that present major problems to the foot traveler. Hikers who have not parked a vehicle at Baldwin Springs should retrace their steps to return to Bartman trailhead.

Distances: To first Fish Pond, 1.4 mi.; to second Fish Pond, 2.5 mi.; to junction of North Bend snowmobile trail, 3.1 mi.; to Baldwin Springs, 6.3 mi. (10.2 km.).

COD POND FROM SHANTY BROOK TRAILHEAD

Cod Pond is small, very attractive and such a short distance from the road that it is a favorite of fishermen, children, and short-distance hikers. Its location at the end of a large vly fed by Stewart Creek makes it home to numerous animals and birds. For nature lovers it is a never-ending series of surprises. Take binoculars and a camera.

To reach the trailhead take NY 30 and turn NE on NY 8, N of Wells. Proceed for 10.1 mi. to the large Shanty Brook parking area on the S (R) side of the road. The trail begins from the SW (R) side of the parking lot. It is also a snowmobile trail marked with showy red disks. A sign says Cod Pond 0.7 mi., North Bend 2.7 mi., Baldwin Springs 4.5 mi. (Posted distances are short by approximately 1.0 mi.)

After the first 75 yds. the trail crosses a tiny stream and turns sharply L to begin climbing a moderate ridge. It continues over numerous rocks and through a wet area, then levels off at 0.2 mi. The trail then descends from the crest to intersect swift-running Stewart Creek at 0.4 mi. The general direction is S. After reaching Stewart Creek, it turns sharply R to cross the creek on a new plank bridge. This very attractive snowmobile bridge is a rich brown color and has been built with railings, too.

After crossing the bridge at this beautiful area, the trail immediately begins an uphill section, soon to reach a trail junction at 0.7 mi. Cod Pond is straight ahead. To reach Baldwin Springs, turn L; this is the old Oregon Trail. (See below.)

A second junction is reached at 0.8 mi. The trail to Cod Pond follows a jog R and, after climbing a small ridge, reaches another trail junction at the crest of the ridge. Here a sign says Cotter Brook is straight ahead, while the Cod Pond trail bends to the L. At 1.2 mi., the trail is well marked with orange snowmobile signs, and the direction is S. The trail surface is level and easy walking. Soon it begins a slight downhill through more open, mature hardwoods.

At 1.3 mi. is another small ridge. The height of land is reached at 1.6 mi. and very soon a large camping area is entered. Here amid the beeches are spots for several tents. Turn L and walk an additional 100 yds. down to the rocky shores of sparkling Cod Pond. There is a picnic rock here, and although the area shows signs of much use, it is usually clean and in good order.

Looking across the pond, the vly can be seen extending into the distant hills. This is an area rich in wildlife, with ducks, otter, muskrat, beaver, deer, bear, coyote, and numerous species of birds and fish living in and around the waters of the pond and surrounding swamplands.

Distances: To Stewart Creek bridge, 0.4 mi.; to first trail junction, 0.7 mi.; to second trail junction, 0.8 mi.; to Cod Pond, 1.7 mi. (2.8 km.).

OREGON TRAIL TO STEWART CREEK FLOW

This is an attractive, easy walk to a small waterfall and picturesque bridge crossing at the site of an old dam. Adventurous hikers may choose to continue and attempt to cross the swamp to rejoin the snowmobile trail on the E side of Stewart Creek Flow, there to walk through seldom-visited pine forests to North Bend and Baldwin Springs.

To reach the beginning of the trail see directions to Cod Pond from Shanty Brook Trailhead above to the first trail junction at 0.7 mi. At that first trail junction, marked with DEC signs, turn L on the Oregon Trail (0 mi.). This trail eventually leads to Baldwin Springs via Stewart Creek Flow and North Bend. (However, Baldwin Springs and North Bend are not recommended to the hiker because it is not feasible to cross Stewart Creek Flow on foot.)

The general direction is E. A small brook is reached and crossed at 0.1 mi. The old roadbed is flat here and passes through open stands of hemlock trees. At 0.4 mi. it bends R; the direction is SSW. It now enters a shallow valley where hemlocks grow on the L and hardwoods on the R. Stewart Creek can be seen on the L at 0.6 mi., flowing slowly because of a beaver dam which comes into sight at 0.8 mi. Just past the dam, the creek rushes around and over a small but attractive waterfall and then around the bend. Here the streambed has been diverted at some point in the past, as evidence to the R and on the trail itself indicates that the stream was once very wide and flowed farther to the R. Beaver have flooded out small trail sections in this area, but all can be skirted to the L or R without much difficulty.

The trail reaches an open area, ascends a little knoll, and then turns sharply L to cross a charming plank bridge at 1.0 mi. at the outlet of Stewart Creek Flow. To the L a stone trough channels the waters to create a rushing flume. There is a picturesque swamp to the R. On the far side of the bridge a series of large boulders that are the remains of a dam provides a convenient resting and picnic place. It is suggested that the walk terminate here, as it has not been possible to cross the vly in recent years during warmer seasons due to extensive flooding by beaver. The trail from here to Baldwin Springs is rough and easily lost because of minimal use by hikers.

Those who do choose to continue can do so by carefully staying to the L of the vly until, after climbing, then descending a small ridge, they reach the edge of the vly at 2.0 mi. Any attempt to bushwhack around this large swampy area to the L and N will take at least an hour or more as the swamp extends for another three-quarters of a mile. Try a turn R and search for and attempt to cross over on the beaver dam, which will be found approximately 0.1 mi. to the R through tall grasses and brush. In recent years the water has been quite high, making this crossing dicey and extremely wet at best.

The hiker who manages to cross the vly will find the trail marked but very wild. This section should be hiked only by those carrying a map and compass. It has been maintained by snowmobile users and so is still discernible. The trail continues with the swamp on the R for another 2.0 mi. to North Bend, and then another 1.9 mi. to Baldwin Springs.

Distances: From Oregon Trail junction (0.7 mi. from the trailhead) to flume and Stewart Creek bridge, 1.7 mi.; to edge of Stewart Creek Flow and flooded crossing, 2.0 mi. (3.2 km.).

PINE ORCHARD AND JIMMY CREEK

Pine Orchard consists of several acres of enormous white pines reputed to be one of the few vestiges of virgin timber left in the Adirondacks. There is no sign to indicate when Pine Orchard has been reached, but the old tote road does pass through the orchard for about a mile. There are several huge pines along both sides of the trail, growing tall and stately, with trunk diameters exceeding six feet quite common.

At least three approaches can be used to reach Pine Orchard. The quickest and easiest walking, by far, is via the Windfall Road entrance near Wells. Here the trail crosses private property, which at this writing is owned by the Flater family, who graciously permit access. A second walk to the orchard begins at the trailhead near

Willis Lake on Pumpkin Hollow Road (see below), and a third alternative is to enter the area via NY 8 where at least two snowmobile trails eventually join to lead into the Pines. However, because this third route traverses wet swamps and is so overgrown, it is not recommended for hiking and has not been included in this trail guide.

To reach Pine Orchard via the Flaters', take NY 30 to Wells. Turn N on Griffin Road, which is directly across from the town beach in Wells. If coming from the S, it is a R turn about 200 yds. before the bridge that crosses Algonquin Lake. If the approach is from the N, make a L immediately after crossing the bridge.

At 0.8 mi. turn R onto Windfall Road. At 1.8 mi. turn R again and continue another 2.0 mi. to the end of this road where signs say "Visitor Parking" on the L and R and announce this to be the private property of the Flaters, where visitors "may need permission to proceed" (0 mi.). If the Flaters are at home, ask permission; if they are not, leave a note with your destination and expected time of return on the car dashboard. Local residents are conscientious and may become concerned if a car remains overly long—therefore backpackers who plan to spend a few days exploring should indicate this.

The trail is a continuation of the now overgrown road. A sturdy barrier bars motor vehicles at 0.2 mi. where the road enters the Forest Preserve. Although the first 0.2 mi. is muddy and rutted by vehicles, the barrier seems to be respected and the road section of the trail beyond is delightfully free of unsightly tracks and mud. A sign says that snowmobiles are permitted in winter.

Immediately after the barrier, a second trail forks R. A sign points the way S to Willis Lake, but the 2.6 mi. is most inaccurate. It is instead over 5 mi. (see below).

The trail descends moderately to 0.6 mi., at which point the waters of a large vly can be seen to the S (R). This is an extension of Taylor Vly, fed by several small streams that eventually join Mill Creek to the E. A small path to the R leads down 0.1 mi. to a rock where the marsh can be viewed.

The main trail reaches the bottom of the ridge, bears R, then crosses a sturdy snowmobile bridge at 0.8 mi. The old road gradually climbs a small ridge until at 1.0 mi. it enters a unique and beautiful corridor of green. In summer, this area is shaded and fringed with lacy greenery created by small spruce, hemlock, and taller white pines with ferns filling in gaps along the lower edges. The trail here is three to four ft. wide, and carpeted with lovely, lush grasses.

A small stream is crossed at 1.4 mi., which then joins a brook paralleling the trail on the R. A clearing with evidence of a camper's fire ring is crossed and the trail then begins to rise moderately. Gradually the white pines have become larger and more numerous and now dominate the landscape. This is Pine Orchard where local residents claim the pines have never been cut. These towering giants serve as reminders of what the forest may have looked like before the intervention of man.

At 1.8 mi. the trail bends L and then R again, climbing the ridge through open glades to enter a second clearing which also has been used as a campsite. The trail turns L again at 2.2 mi. and descends towards the marsh, which can be seen on the R. Although the trail still traverses an open pine forest, the trees here are younger and smaller. The giants of Pine Orchard have been passed.

The trail becomes narrower and less traveled as it skirts the edge of the vly, becoming rough and much more difficult to walk. Although there are only a few small wet areas, at 2.6 mi. a rather swampy section with wet, moss-covered rocks leads deceptively into wetter, grass-covered muck. The hiker should go to the R through some low brush to avoid this, rejoining the main path about 250 ft. beyond. Continue N and cross a small brook at 2.8 mi.

The beautiful old road is now a small path which at times becomes a challenge to find, especially amid the lush growth of summer or in late fall after the leaves have fallen. Snowmobile signs are posted, but not frequently enough to reassure the novice hiker. From here on a map and compass should be carried and frequently consulted.

The path climbs a ridge at 3.0 mi. At the top an open hardwood forest begins. Here the path fades and can easily be lost; it dips to the NE at approximately 60 degrees magnetic N and reappears on the other side of a large fallen pine, then continues up the next small ridge. Look for a faded marker on the R near the top of this ridge. At the top the trail becomes better marked with two shiny orange snowmobile disks and then several faded ones in the next mile.

At this writing (1985), there are numerous blowdowns and scant evidence of human use for any purpose. (This is certainly a walk on the wild side for those so inclined.) At 3.7 mi., after a series of rolling ridges, the trail bears S but at 3.8 mi. two DEC arrows direct one L (NE) again. Another unnamed stream is crossed at 3.9 mi. Up the bank about 500 yds. there appears on the R a dark brown privy. Decaying split firewood is neatly stacked on the L, and there is a permanent fireplace made with cemented stones. A brown and yellow DEC sign, "If you carry it in, carry it out," indicates that this is a state designated camping area. A large plastic container is tipped on its side and several plastic tarps and other debris are scattered about, but there is no evidence of recent use, as the site is quite overgrown and the firewood is sprouting bracket fungi.

At 4.5 mi. an attractive rock ledge approximately 15 ft. high is seen on the R, and at 4.8 mi. Jimmy Creek is reached. The snowmobile bridge that once spanned this rocky creek bed now lies shattered beneath a huge fallen birch.

Hikers who have come this far and wish to continue should be aware that the snowmobile trail proceeds through Cotter Swamp before branching off to the W (L) in two places to join trails going to NY 8. Add another 3 to 4 more miles if the through trip is to be completed. A through trip is not recommended. Getting through the swamp will be wet, and possibly dangerous in any season other than winter.

Distances: To snowmobile bridge, 0.8 mi.; to Pine Orchard, approximately 1.6 mi.; to ridge, 3.0 mi.; to Jimmy Creek and washed-out snowmobile bridge, 4.8 mi. (7.8 km.).

PINE ORCHARD FROM PUMPKIN HOLLOW ROAD

This is a long walk through seldom-visited wild forests. Though it follows a snowmobile trail, it is an adventure to be undertaken only by those who want practice in trail-following and map and compass reading, for the trail fades in several areas.

To reach the trailhead, take NY 30 and turn N (R) on Pumpkin Hollow Road (S of Wells) at 0.1 mi. after passing a large white building currently (1986) housing a restaurant. Continue 1.6 mi. up Pumpkin Hollow Road to the trailhead, which begins on the N (L) where large guideboards point the way. There is parking on the L and R shoulders of the road. This is also the beginning of the trail to Murphy, Middle and Bennett Lakes to the S (R). (See below.)

The DEC sign obviously has been corrected to read 5.0 mi. to Pine Orchard. However, it is 5.0 mi. to the junction of an old tote road that leads another 1.6 mi. into the Pine Orchard, a total of 6.6 mi. (See above.)

The trail begins from the Willis Lake/Pumpkin Hollow trailhead and proceeds through a young pine forest. The original trail was rerouted to avoid private property around Willis Lake; thus for the first 0.5 mi. it leads N, passing a small pond on the R, then crosses a footbridge and passes below two privately owned camps on the hill to the R. At 0.5 mi. an intersection is well marked by a trail sign on the R and a big white pine on the L, where the trail now joins the old farm road and proceeds N (L) towards Coulombe Creek.

The trail provides easy walking through a mature forest of mixed pines. It is covered with pine needles, and the grades are gentle. A bend to the R (E) at 1.2 mi. takes the hiker along the side of an openly wooded ridge, then down and across a small creek. A series of small grades is encountered and the old road becomes rocky and eroded in many places. Several fallen trees lie across the trail at 1.6 mi., after which it becomes more level and then makes a gradual turn to the N.

The impressive foundations of the barn of an old farmstead lie to the L and R of the trail at 1.9 mi. Descend through a wet area and up a small rise, and look to the R at 2.0 mi. to observe the square foundation of the tiny farm house. Continue along this old road for another 0.4 mi. until Coulombe Creek is crossed. The old road the trail has been following apparently ended at the creek. From here to the junction of the trail into Pine Orchard, the hiker should carry a compass and know how to read it. After crossing the creek this trail becomes a mere overgrown path, rough and very poorly defined and marked.

The trail now enters and crosses an overgrown clearing, and for the next two mi. it climbs and descends numerous ridges, often becoming rock-strewn and difficult to walk, and to find. Snowmobile signs are infrequent.

At 3.8 mi. a turn E (R) and up a knoll is indicated by bright orange snowmobile disks. Although the trail is somewhat obscure, when the top of the knoll is reached, watch for a long, flat rocky ridge on the L that rises above this small valley. This is a picturesque section.

A flat rock clearing is reached at 4.1 mi. It is shaded by trees and is high enough to catch a breeze in the heat of summer—a good spot to take a break. (This will no doubt come to be known as "Dog-in-the-Tree Clearing" because in 1984 or 1985 someone tied a four-foot stuffed toy dog in a big pine tree. The remains will hang there until they disintegrate!)

Leaving "Dog-in-the-Tree Clearing," the path continues E through mixed hardwoods, then descends over more rocks, travels through an evergreen thicket and finally, at 5.0 mi., intersects the old tote road leading to Pine Orchard. Turn R and follow this easy section mostly downhill for another 1.6 mi. into the heart of Pine Orchard. (See trail description for Pine Orchard and Jimmy Creek, above.)

This is a long walk (12 to 14 mi. round trip) for the hiking group that does not leave a car at the trailhead near the Flaters' off Windfall Road. (See above.) Due to the poor condition of the trail and disuse by hikers of the section between the old farm ruins on Coulombe Creek and the old road through Pine Orchard, it is not recommended that anyone hike this section without a group of at least three persons and prior knowledge of, and experience in, the use of map and compass.

Distances: To ruins of old farmstead, 1.9 mi.; to Coulombe Creek crossing, 2.4 mi.; to old road, 5.0 mi.; to Pine Orchard, 6.6 mi. (10.6 km.).

MURPHY LAKE FROM PUMPKIN HOLLOW ROAD

Murphy Lake is charming, surrounded by small foothills, with rocky cliffs to the N and W lending an air of unlimited adventures to the day's outing. A bushwhack up the ridge to either cliff top is feasible, with care. For most hikers, though, the moderate trail walk through attractive stretches of hardwoods and evergreens, along creeks and past beaver meadows and ponds, will more than satisfy. A through trip of a little over eight miles can be made around Murphy, then past Middle and Bennett Lakes, making this one of the nicest day hikes in the southern Adirondacks. (See Murphy Lake from Creek Road below, for directions to the other end of the trail.)

The trail, for the most part, follows an ancient road used by the early settlers of the region as a main N/S route. Farms once occupied the valleys and one can still find stone foundations, as well as ancient apple trees, on occasion.

To reach the trailhead drive N on Route 30 along the Sacandaga River and turn R onto Pumpkin Hollow Road, which is 0.3 mi. after a sign that says Town of Wells near a large building currently (1986) housing a restaurant. Continue driving on Pumpkin Hollow Road for 1.6 mi.—mostly uphill—until the DEC trail markers are seen on the L. Parking is available for several vehicles on both sides of the road, although in the spring the shoulders are extremely soft.

The yellow-marked trail for Murphy Lake begins on the R through a pine plantation consisting of mature white pines and hemlocks. The trail register is encountered immediately as the hiker enters the forest. Heading in a S direction, the trail turns L at 0.2 mi. Now heading E, the trail begins to descend a short but steep ridge. At 0.3 mi. a bend L occurs and the trail passes through a wet area at the bottom of the hill. This trail is well marked with snowmobile signs as well as yellow DEC hiking trail signs.

The trail continues through a thicket of hemlocks, scattered white pines, and spruce until at 0.4 mi. it reaches a corduroy boardwalk of rounded logs spanning a swampy area for approximately 50 yds. At 0.5 mi. the trail leaves the swamp and goes through an avenue lined with green pines, their needles making the trail surface soft and pleasant. This is a beautiful area, flat and easy walking. Note the yellow state-land boundary marks on the trees to the R.

The trail begins a descent at 0.65 mi. and then passes through a rocky, wet area at 0.7 mi. At the bottom of this small ridge a little wooden bridge spans a marshy area. That is shortly followed by a section of densely laid rocks over more small wet sections.

A curve R at 0.9 mi. leads shortly to a trail junction. Bear L. To the R is private land, the continuation of the old road back to Pumpkin Hollow. At 1.1 mi. the trail bends sharply L. The trail is now part of the remains of the historic old road that served the farms along the way. A barrier restricting access to motorized vehicles is reached after crossing another swampy area on a series of dual split-log bridges.

Now the trail is flat as the evergreens begin to give way to deciduous trees. A fairly steep descent begins, traversing a rocky, washed-out gully that once was a road. At the bottom a wood-plank snowmobile bridge crosses a medium-sized stream.

At 1.6 mi. the forest has changed to a more open woods of ash, birch, and maple. Wildflowers are abundant here, especially in spring. At 1.8 mi. another wet area is spanned by planks. A major wood bridge crosses over large Doig Creek at 1.9 mi. On the other side of the bridge the trail is usually wet and muddy, thanks to the flooding by beaver upstream which has changed part of the flow.

After the wet area, the trail climbs a ridge. It now passes through a very washed-out area. A check to the L in this vicinity will reveal the stone foundation ruins of an old building as well as an apple tree here and there, the remains of an old farm orchard.

At 2.3 mi. another moderate uphill begins as the forest changes to more open hardwoods. Top a small rise at 2.4 mi. and note to the L an old beaver meadow, which may be flooded anew by beaver. Another sturdy bridge is reached; it has recently been flooded by beaver who built a dam against the bridge. Note that there are two dams, one abutting the bridge on the L and another about 50 yds. into the pond.

The trail now begins to follow the creek upstream toward the outlet of Murphy Lake. Note the enormous pine at 2.9 mi. It is obviously a survivor of the original logging days, due, perhaps, to its position on the stream bank at the side of the road.

The trail continues up a small ridge. At 3.4 mi. the outlet creek must be crossed. The bridge that spanned this shallow but swift-flowing section of creek has been washed out, and during spring and other high-water times the hiker may have to go upstream, or down, to find a suitable crossing spot.

After crossing the outlet stream, the trail goes through and up a small, very attractive ravine covered with moss and cascades of ferns. As the trail exits the ravine, notice the pink boulder on the R. The trail continues to follow the stream until the outlet of Murphy Lake is reached at 3.8 mi.

The trail continues to circle Murphy Lake to the L (N) for another three-quarters of a mile to the lean-to on its E end. Just before the lean-to, however, it is necessary to turn L (N) again and circle around a wet section created by a beaver dam that has raised the lake level by at least a foot, backing up the water and flooding the original trail.

The lean-to, only a few years old, is located on a knoll sheltered by large white pines and attractive boulders. (The original lean-to was burned by careless hikers in the late 1970s.) This has been a favorite camping area for hunters, hikers, skiers and snowmobilers for many years.

The trail continues from the lean-to to the E and up a ridge for another half-mile to Middle Lake.

Distances: To junction of old road and barrier, 1.1 mi.; to Doig Creek bridge, 1.8.mi.; to beaver dam and bridge, 2.5 mi.; to Murphy Lake outlet, 3.8 mi.; to lean-to on Murphy Lake, 4.5 mi. (7.1 km.).

MURPHY LAKE FROM CREEK ROAD

Murphy, Middle and Bennett Lakes lie along an ancient road which has been in use for well over 100 years. Perhaps it was even used by the Indians prior to the early farmers who attempted to till the area. Along sections of the trail you can still identify ancient apple trees and the stone foundations and cellar holes of homes and barns.

To reach the trailhead, take NY 30 N from Mayfield. After crossing the bridge over the Sacandaga River at Benson, drive another 4.1 mi. and turn R onto Creek Road. Proceed up Creek Road for 2.5 mi. to the trailhead on the L (N), marked with DEC brown and yellow guideboards. Park on either side of the road; the shoulders are very wide.

The trail begins on the N side of the road, through a thick forest of mixed evergreens and hardwoods. A wood plank bridge spans a small stream and wet area at 0.1 mi. and then the trail begins to climb a ridge—moderately, for the most part, with a few steeper sections, using the old washed-out roadbed. In places it is very rocky and rough underfoot.

At 0.6 mi., after passing through a lovely avenue of white pines, look to the L to see an ancient stone wall. There is a substantial iron barrier to discourage motorized traffic at the top of the ridge at 0.8 mi. The trail descends for about 75 yds., then jogs sharply R, although it appears at first glance to continue straight ahead.

At the top of the small rise at 1.0 mi. the trail passes over an area of dark red soil. There is also a depression on the L. This is all that remains of a settlement and ferric oxide mine which produced pigments used to make paint at the turn of the century. No readily visible evidence remains, although exploration will uncover cellar holes and occasional iron scraps of machinery and stoves—the forest has reclaimed the land.

The trail climbs moderately in a NNW direction through lovely open hardwoods and mixed evergreens. The old road is often illegally used by ATVs and is wet and mucky in some sections as it continues a moderate uphill until at 1.3 mi. a fork goes off the the R. This unmarked path leads 0.4 mi. down the ridge to the shore of Bennett Lake, which in fall and winter can be glimpsed through the trees. There are two or three open camping areas, well-used, but attractive. The main trail, however, continues to follow the contours of the ridge, about a quarter of a mile above the lakeshore.

At 1.6 mi. a steeper and rocky section is reached. A faint cutoff to the R has been created by motorized vehicles to avoid the rocky ravine, but it is hardly necessary for the hiker. At 1.7 mi. the main trail reaches a stream with a sturdy plank snowmobile bridge across it. After crossing it, the trail bends R and up, making a few snake-like turns.

At 2.2 mi. the trail passes through a picturesque ravine and at 2.3 mi. reaches a small stream that does not have a bridge. It can, however, be crossed on rocks or a convenient log.

At 2.4 mi. the trail traverses a level section, and then bends R. It is very smooth and easy to walk, very attractive. A cutoff to the R that goes to a camping area on the shore of Middle Lake occurs at 2.6 mi., and the lake itself comes into view shortly thereafter. The trail continues along the ridge approximately 200 ft. from the lakeshore, until at 3.0 mi. a path to the R leads to the water. From here Middle Lake's island can be seen, as can the attractive rocks on the E shore.

Middle Lake, although shallow, is charming. If time permits, a bushwhack to the E shore will provide many attractive scenes and picnic spots.

At the N end of Middle Lake, the trail comes very close to the water, then leaves its shores to continue in a general NW direction towards Murphy Lake. A short but steep climb up a small hill occurs, and then the trail begins a moderate descent at 3.5 mi. through a quiet, densely overgrown section of the forest. The trail itself, however, is grass-covered and smooth underfoot.

At 3.6 mi. a large mucky area must be negotiated, and at 3.7 mi. the shores of Murphy Lake come into view. The lean-to on its shore is reached at 3.8 mi.

Murphy Lake is situated in a bowl between three small mountains, with dramatic bare cliffs lending an air of ruggedness to the scene. Large boulders decorate its shoreline, and the knoll upon which the new lean-to sits is shaded by huge white pines.

Distances: To iron barrier, 0.8 mi.; to path to Bennett Lake shore, 1.3.; to Middle Lake, 2.6 mi.; to Murphy Lake and lean-to, 3.8 mi. (6.2 km.).

CATHEAD MT.

A hike up Cathead Mt. offers a number of rewards, considering the shortness of the climb to the summit (1.6 mi.). This small mountain, 2423 ft. in elevation, is also an excellent choice for the snowshoer who wants practice for more demanding trips. On a clear day, the bare summit offers outstanding views of the surrounding countryside; one can often see the High Peaks to the N. At this writing it is still one of the few Adirondack mountains with a manned fire tower. The tower has recently been enhanced (or defaced, according to one's interpretation) by the addition of a radio tower extension for use by the New York State Police. This has also necessitated the construction of a beige, aluminum outbuilding on the W side of the summit to house radio equipment. Despite this, the views are still outstanding to the N, E, and S, and from the tower in all four directions.

To reach the trailhead take NY 30 and turn W on to Benson Road. (If you are coming from the S it is a L turn.) A brown and yellow DEC trail sign marks the entrance to this road. Travel 2.7 mi. and turn R on North Road, which is also marked with a DEC trail sign. Proceed to the end of this dirt road traveling a little over 1.0 mi. and park to the R in a small parking area. Be careful not to block the driveway on the L, as parking is adequate here for only two or three cars, and all others will have to park along the shoulders of the road.

The trail begins straight ahead along the chained-off extension of the road which is marked by a Private Road sign. Walk 250 yds. along this road and turn sharply L where a sign tacked to a big white pine indicates 1.25 mi. to Cathead Mt. The trail follows the observer's telephone line up a well-defined path through a cleared right-of-way in the woods.

At 0.3 mi. a split-log footbridge crosses over a small stream and in another 40 yds. a similar bridge crosses a second fork of the stream. At 0.5 mi. the climb becomes steeper and continues NNW through attractive hardwoods—oak, ash, maple and beech—still following the telephone line. At 0.8 mi. a series of steeper areas, interspersed with short level sections, begins. These natural terraces contain colorful wildflowers, especially in spring when the trout lily is in bloom.

After a slight jog L at 0.9 mi., the trail traverses a steep, extremely rocky area. This section, with its unstable footing, becomes a watercourse during rainy weather and snowmelt. The trail becomes moderately steep at 1.1 mi. and is often scoured to bedrock. At 1.3 mi. it reaches a flat area, and at 1.5 mi. the tower comes into view, with the observer's cabin located on a level area right below the summit. The trail continues to the R of the attractive brown cabin and then climbs steeply for another one-tenth of a mile to the summit and tower.

On the summit a 270-degree panoramic view provides ample rewards for the effort expended. The tower is also accessible for views to all points.

Distances: To level terraces with views, 0.8 mi.; to observer's cabin, 1.5 mi.; to summit, 1.6 mi. (2.6 km.). Ascent, 1273 ft. (389 m.). Elevation, 2427 ft. (442 m.).

East Canada Creek

CHASE LAKE

A pretty, popular lake with a lean-to, Chase Lake is visited frequently by ATV riders and as a result sections of the trail may be wet and muddy. Nevertheless, it is an interesting destination for the hiker who enjoys walking old roads.

Take the Benson Road, turning W off NY 30 or E off NY 10 if coming from the W. Turn N on Pinnacle Road and drive 2.6 mi. to the end of this dirt road where parking for two or three cars is available at the turnaround. The trail begins to the E (R) of the turnaround and is well marked as a snowmobile route. It is also occasionally marked with the smaller bright yellow DEC foot trail disks.

A swampy area must be crossed at 0.1 mi. This wet section needs to be crossed carefully on small logs and grass tufts. It is not feasible to go around it, as it extends quite a distance both N and S.

The trail heads E but soon turns N (L) on an old logging road. At 0.3 mi. a jog to the R occurs and the trail continues through more muck, then crosses a small stream. The next section is easy walking; the trail meanders through small curves to the L, then R. It enters a stand of young beeches with several dead larger ones strewn about the landscape. At 0.4 mi. the trail begins to climb a small hill, then bends gently to the R. Very soon the hill is topped and a gentle descent commences at 0.5 mi. Here the trail enters a section of hemlocks—a dark contrast to the high forests of birch and beech.

Twisting and turning at 0.6 mi. but still easy to follow, the trail begins a downhill section. After a brief but steep descent, it crosses a larger stream on a snowmobile bridge at 0.8 mi. and then makes a jog L.

An extensive carpet of lovely tree clubmoss is passed at 0.9 mi. These mosses, which look like miniature, shiny evergreen trees, once were much more common, but they have been removed for decades for holiday decorations and now are protected by law.

At 1.0 mi. the general direction is S. The trail passes through another grove of hemlocks where it would be easy to lose except that some enterprising person has tacked bright pink and orange plastic rectangles on several trees. At 1.1 mi. the trail joins another old logging road. The trail turns E (L) on this road. From here to Chase Lake it follows this wide, occasionally muddy road which shows signs of intensive ATV use. Sections of it have become permanent water/mud holes, but all can be skirted easily to the L or R, and in several sections the road is high, dry and flat—very pleasant to walk. The woods are mature and open and there are numerous species of wildflowers to be seen, especially in spring.

At 1.3 mi. a small creek is crossed on rocks and old boards, and another, larger one is encountered at 1.4 mi. This one is crossed on a solid wood plank bridge. Several twists and turns occur at 2.0 mi., as well as a few minor undulations. The general direction is still E. The waters of Chase Lake are sighted at 2.3 mi., and the trail reaches the lean-to at 2.5 mi. after a brief downhill jog.

Chase Lake is very pretty, but access to the water is restricted by the swampy, boggy shoreline. Even at the lean-to, access to the lake must be made through a wet and muddy track. Because the road makes it easily accessible by motorized vehicles, the lean-to is overused and, unfortunately, its beauty is marred by cans, plastic and other trash. Occasionally some visitors do carry out trash, because this writer found it much cleaner on the second visit than the first.

A circle trip on trails is not possible, so the hiker is advised to return the same way although one can follow the old logging roads for many miles. A reminder: Carry a map and compass when exploring this and any other unfamiliar area.

Distances: To hemlock grove with pink signs, 1.0 mi.; to junction of logging (ATV) road, 1.1 mi.; to Chase Lake and lean-to, 2.5 mi. (4.1 km.).

DUNNING POND FROM NY 30

Primarily a snowmobile route to Gilmantown Road over an old road, this walk leads the hiker through some very wild sections. Apparently little used by snowmobilers, probably because it isn't very long for them, the trail is a challenge. It is so overgrown and hidden by blowdown and beaver flooding that it should be undertaken only by the experienced bushwhacker. Map and compass are a must.

To reach the E trailhead take NY 30, N through Wells. At the N end of town, a sharp curve to the R must be executed. At 3.1 mi. from this curve, a DEC yellow and brown trail sign on the L is easily observed from the highway. Park on the shoulders of NY 30, either side, as this is a wide, flat section. One may also turn L and drive up the embankment on the dirt road; however, the tiny parking area among the trees will accommodate only one or two cars at the most, before the barrier is reached at 0.1 mi.

The DEC sign reads Dunning Pond 3.4 mi. and Gilmantown Road 4.3 mi. The distances are actually considerably longer for the hiker due to the need to circumvent swamps, a beaver dam and a number of fallen trees—at least during the summer of 1985. Note also that Dunning Pond has now become "Dunning Swamp." Nevertheless, although the trail is wildly overgrown and there are stretches of difficult walking due to rocks exposed on washed-out sections, parts of this walk are lovely and worth the effort to explore. An impressive beaver dam and pond will be encountered at 3.2 mi. and the casual hiker may wish to terminate the trip there.

Past the sturdy steel barrier that bars motor vehicles during all but the winter months, the road begins a gentle climb through a mixed forest of hemlock and several species of hardwoods. On the L is Dunning Creek, but at 0.5 mi. the road curves NW and leaves the creek to climb higher on the ridge. For the rest of the first mile the road is a series of ups and downs but always climbing higher up the shoulder of the unnamed mountain on the R. Finally at 1.2 mi. it enters a clearing and then descends briefly to parallel a small stream, which it crosses in another 50 ft. (During low water, rock-hopping in the stream bed will be easy.)

The road climbs up a rocky washout, then turns L to traverse a flat, curved section of the ridge. On the L is a very steep ravine banked by mature hemlocks. The creek far below can be heard but not seen.

At 1.7 mi. the top of the ridge is reached and the path becomes smooth and pleasant. After another small uphill grade, it crosses a second small stream at 2.2 mi. Gradually, evidence of the road disappears; but the footpath is still easy to follow, although it is poorly marked at long intervals with snowmobile signs and marked not at all with foot trail signs.

The descent now begins, heading W at 2.5 mi. over a series of dips and level areas. An enormous upraised multiple tree root system is seen on the R at 2.9 mi. at the bottom of a col. This interesting tangle is the result of the trees' growth in an extremely shallow layer of soil. The underlying rocks are now exposed to create a mossy, rocky and damp area. Rock-hopping these, the hiker will find that the path descends to the creek at 3.2 mi. through a beautiful open section of mature trees.

The creek has been dammed 75 ft. upstream on the R by beaver. At this writing the dam is 3 ft. high and in excellent condition, creating a large pond which the continuing hiker will have to circumvent. A fishermen's path to the R can be used to investigate the beaver dam, but it disappears very quickly. The marked snowmobile trail crosses the creek and continues SW upsteam, disappearing into the pond. The snowmobile bridge has been washed out by spring floods and lies partially on the L bank (looking downstream) across the path. In spring the creek may be impossible to cross due to high water, but the many rocks exposed during summer and fall permit easy access to the opposite bank.

After crossing Dunning Creek, the hiker must keep to the L bank of the pond, pushing through about 50 ft. of spruce scrub and generally bushwhacking through brush and blowdown and wet areas, until at 3.5 mi. the trail reappears where the creek enters the newly created pond.

The trail continues along the creek, passing a pretty three-tier waterfall approximately 15 ft. high at 3.9 mi. Still heading SW along the creek, the trail provides vistas of an older beaver pond now turned into a meadow. The path rises to join again with the vestiges of an old tote road at 4.1 mi., now heading W. Here it is once again easy walking on the smoother roadbed, and here too, down the ridge to the R, lies the swamp which is all that remains of Dunning Pond. In summer one can catch a glimpse through the trees of quiet waters spotted with yellow bullhead lilies, and at other seasons it is possible to see in detail the last remains of a pond returned to marshland.

Distances: To beaver dam, 3.2 mi.; to waterfall, 3.9 mi.; to Dunning Pond, 4.2 mi. (6.8 km.).

DUNNING POND FROM GILMANTOWN ROAD

This is a short walk to an interesting pond that is in the final transition to a swamp. The trail traverses an old road and can also be made into a 5-mi. through trip to NY 30, just above Wells. (See Dunning Pond from NY 30, above.)

Approaching from the W, turn N on Gilmantown Road (which leaves NY 30 0.2 miles W of the Algonquin Lake bridge in Wells). The beginning of the trail is on the R 3.8 mi. from Wells. (Or 0.5 mi. past Charley Lake.) A small creek runs out of the trail and down the embankment into the ditch in wetter seasons. A small plank bridge crosses the ditch, and a brown and yellow DEC trail sign can be found partially hidden by the trees. It is, however, difficult to spot from the road. There is ample parking along both shoulders of Gilmantown Road.

This is the continuation of an old wagon road, with evidence that at one time it was deeply rutted. At 0.4 mi. the trail begins a slight descent; at this writing it has a great deal of blowdown scattered across several sections. The woods are composed predominantly of hardwoods, and many species of ferns and wildflowers, as well as the attractive staghorn moss, can be found.

At 0.6 mi. the trail turns slightly to the L. The average hiker will have no trouble following this broad old roadbed even though it is poorly marked. Still heavily eroded, the path is rocky and rough in several places.

A jog R occurs at 1.0 mi., and Dunning Pond comes into sight through the trees to the L. At 1.2 mi. watch for a blaze on a tree on the L and then a big orange snowmobile disk on another nearby tree. Cut to the L, then continue down to the W end of the pond to the outlet where there is a small camping area. Large old hemlocks grace the banks of this small pond, which has been enlarged and temporarily deepened by beaver activity. It is pleasant and attractive, although in the final stages of the gradual transition into a swampy Adirondack bog.

Distances: To view of Dunning Pond, 1.0 mi.; to path to pond, 1.2 mi. (1.9 km.).

WHITEHOUSE TO BIG EDDY

Big Eddy is a popular, quiet area along the West Branch of the Sacandaga River, where the waters rest after a violent cascade through the West Branch Gorge. The walk is easy and filled with scenic woods and streams.

To reach the trailhead turn W off NY 30 in the town of Wells, onto

Algonquin Drive, then L on West River Road. Follow this road 8.0 mi. to Whitehouse and the trailhead. Whitehouse was a settlement, then a hunting camp during the 1950s, and is now a large clearing gradually reverting to forest. There is plenty of parking space and several popular campsites in addition to the foundations and chimneys of former buildings.

The trail begins from the clearing at the end of the dirt road, heading generally W to the trail register at 0.1 mi. at the junction of the Northville-Placid (N-P) Trail.

The trail is an old road, still quite wide, smooth, and easy to walk, going in a NNW direction. A small stream is crossed at 0.3 mi. and at 0.5 mi. the road takes a slight jog to the R and continues through pleasant hardwoods interspersed with occasional hemlocks and pines.

The road/trail reaches a junction at 0.7 mi. The N-P Trail continues R (N) towards Piseco, and the old road meanders WNW towards the confluence of Hamilton Lake Stream (a major inlet of the Sacandaga) and the West Branch of the Sacandaga. At 1.1 mi. Hamilton Lake Stream comes into sight on the R, and the trail continues down an incline to a large clearing at 1.2 mi. This clearing is frequently used as a camping area and has several logs and rocks strategically located by previous campers. The area is clean and attractive, and has been used for forty or fifty years as a campsite. Until the late fifties, the old farm road was negotiable by rugged vehicles up to this point. Now, illegal ATVs ply the woods.

Here the hiker can most easily cross Hamilton Lake Stream, although in the spring, especially, one must be prepared to wade. Although the stream is shallow and gently flowing with numerous rocks in the stream bed, only during a dry midsummer hike is one likely to find sufficient exposed logs or boulders to rock-hop it. Plan on a possibly dicey stroll through icy waters with slippery rocks underfoot.

After crossing the stream, the well-beaten fishermen's path turns

L in a WSW direction, passing through avenues of mature hard-woods. At 1.3 mi. the banks of the West Branch of the Sacandaga come into sight. The path is occasionally obscured by vegetation and fallen trees, but it is merely a matter of following the stream bank to Big Eddy. The West Branch of the Sacandaga is a fast-flowing stream at this point, cavorting over numerous rocks that create sometimes spectacular rapids. Big Eddy, in contrast, is a quiet, peaceful section of the stream, occurring immediately after the water's violent cascade through the gorge.

Finally, after winding over many large rocks and granite outcrop-pings, always hugging the N shore, the path enters the West Branch Gorge. Footing is difficult, and the hiker is urged to take great care since the water cascades through the gorge at a tremendous velocity, especially in spring. In fact, it is not recommended that one even enter the gorge then. A glimpse of the powerful flow can also be had from the top of the cliff to the R. To reach this vantage point, it is suggested that the hiker veer away from the stream before the actual need to scale the steep slopes, and take the more gradually inclined ridge on the eastern side. Hikers are urged to use a compass and carry a topographic map should they decide to climb to the top.

Distances: To Hamilton Lake Stream crossing, 1.2 mi.; to banks of West Branch of the Sacandaga, 1.4 mi.; to Big Eddy, 2.0 mi.; (3.2 km.).

NORTHVILLE-PLACID TRAIL
FROM PISECO TO UPPER BENSON (N TO S)

PISECO (NY 8) TO WHITEHOUSE

The southern section of the 132.2 mi. Northville-Placid Trail (N-P Trail) cuts through the center of the southern Adirondack forest known as The Silver Lake Wilderness. The entire trail is described in

Guide to Adirondack Trails: Northville-Placid Trail, published by the Adirondack Mountain Club (1986). The section described here is 25.3 mi. long and includes some of the wildest, most interesting hiking in the southern Adirondacks. To do the hike as a through trip from one end to the other, one should allow a minimum of two days and one overnight—ideally, three days and two overnights—to permit sufficient time to enjoy the scenery and explore side trails.

The section of the N-P Trail from Piseco to Upper Benson via Whitehouse begins on the S side of NY 8 at the Arietta Highway Department garage, across from a general store. A brown and yellow DEC sign indicates that the Hamilton Lake Stream Lean-to is 3.6 mi., Whitehouse, 6.4 mi.

The trail, which is well marked with blue DEC trail disks, starts in the trees to the W of the garage and within 50 yds. bears R up a small hill, then goes through an open field. It enters the forest, passing the trail register at 0.2 mi. A moderate uphill climb commences through a predominantly deciduous forest; the path is wide and pleasant to walk. Two small streams are crossed, one and then another a few feet farther, at 0.5 mi. The trail direction is S. A jog R at 1.0 mi. and then a climb brings the hiker to the crest of a ridge.

Buckhorn Lake's outlet stream is reached at 1.1 mi. The hiker crosses on a dual-log bridge with handrails and then turns slightly to the R. After a rocky section at 1.2 mi., the trail curves R and up a moderate grade. A mucky spot must be traversed at 1.6 mi. although, in general, the trail is very pleasant to walk. The general direction is E as the path descends at 2.0 mi. and crosses a large stream at 2.3 mi. There is an impressive beaver dam at 2.4 mi., and it appears it was very recently washed out. The pond behind it is gone, leaving an unsightly mud meadow.

A large vly is now seen to the L—Priests Vly—with a major stream at 2.5 mi. flowing out of it. At 2.8 mi. the trail crosses a small stream, and another at 2.9 mi. The trail continues along the bank of yet another stream, and at 3.1 mi. descends a moderate ridge. It crosses a swifter stream at 3.3 mi. and rises to the top of a knoll where a sign points to the Hamilton Lake Stream lean-to on the L. Turn L here. In one-tenth of a mile the Hamilton Lake Stream Lean-to is reached.

This lean-to sits on a knoll above a small stream that joins Hamilton Lake Stream farther E. The hiker must descend a steep bank to get to it. The stream can be seen easily from the front of the lean-to. Although this is a pleasant, attractive site, it is overused, with most vegetation trampled and absent over a larger-than-normal area.

Leaving the lean-to, the trail passes through hardwoods mixed with evergreens and quickly descends to a small swampy section that is easily traversed on a split-log boardwalk. This lowland area is sunny and open and the hiker can observe numerous attractive flowers and swamp plants during the warmer seasons. Leaving the swamp, the trail immediately crosses a tiny stream on another little plank bridge.

A suspension bridge crossing Hamilton Lake Stream is reached at 3.7 mi. There is an open camping area on the stream bank. The trail continues E, descending into a wet section at 3.9 mi. For the next mile the trail traverses the rich lowland deciduous forest, an easy, pleasant section.

At 5.1 mi. it crosses another stream and again, at 5.5 mi. At 5.6 mi. the trail reaches an old tote road to Whitehouse. A R (W) turn at this junction leads to Big Eddy and the gorge of the West Branch of the Sacandaga. (Big Eddy is a quiet area of the West Branch that occurs just after the waters rush violently through the gorge; see above.)

Turn L (E). The next mile to Whitehouse is flat, easy, and pleasant walking along the old road. The woods are open, with some mixed evergreens, but mostly hardwoods. Grasses and ferns are in abundance. The trail register at Whitehouse is reached at 6.6 mi.

Distances: To outlet of Buckhorn Lake, 1.1 mi.; to Priests Vly, 2.5 mi.; to Hamilton Lake Stream Lean-to, 3.4 mi.; to Hamilton Lake Stream suspension bridge, 3.7 mi.; to trail junction to Big Eddy, 5.6 mi.; to Whitehouse, 6.6 mi. (10.7 km.).

NORTHVILLE-PLACID TRAIL
FROM PISECO TO UPPER BENSON (N TO S)

WHITEHOUSE TO SILVER LAKE;
SILVER LAKE TO UPPER BENSON

Note: Mileage is given cumulatively from Whitehouse to Upper Benson since Silver Lake is not accessible to begin a hike.

For driving directions to Whitehouse see Whitehouse to Big Eddy trail description above. Hikers heading S to Silver Lake from Whitehouse would walk W from the unpaved parking area for 0.4 mi. along a dirt track and take a L at the junction where the trail register is located.

Hikers coming from Piseco should stop to explore the ruins of Whitehouse. To do so, continue straight (E) at the register for another 0.4 mi. to the clearing where cars can be parked. Wander about the area and note the stone foundations—and one impressive stone chimney—of the homes and buildings once located here. Many were used as hunting camps until the late 1940s.

For the through hiker, the trail turns S (R) at the register and descends to the banks of the West Branch and the suspension bridge. Notice the fireplace ruins directly in front of the bridge, all that remains of a boys' camp recreation hall. Cross the West Branch on the suspension bridge—a "swinging" experience! The trail turns sharply L and follows the West Branch for approximately 150 ft., then turns S. Take care to follow the blue trail signs, as there are other well-used trails going both directions along the stream banks.

The trail for the first 1.0 mi. is easy and pleasant to follow through mixed deciduous trees and evergreens. A small stream is crossed at 1.4 mi. Immediately thereafter the trail reaches a junction and a yellow and brown DEC trail sign pointing the hiker to the R for the N-P Trail. The path L returns to the West Branch.

The trail crosses a bog on a plank bridge and begins climbing at 1.6 mi. through a rather rocky and moderately steep section. At 1.8 mi. the trail bears L slightly and continues through hardwoods until it crosses another bog on a split-log bridge. The trail now begins to climb moderately.

At 2.0 mi. it reaches the crest of a ridge and at 2.2 mi. a wet area must be skirted. The trail then begins to climb a long, steep ridge. The top of this ridge is reached at 2.7 mi. Two small streams are crossed, and the trail meanders through mostly level terrain until at 2.9 mi. a part of the marsh that surrounds Mud Lake is encountered. At 3.0 mi. Mud Lake Lean-to is reached. Here a DEC sign says Canary Pond 3.25 mi.; Silver Lake Lean-to 5.9 mi.; and Northville 23.6 mi.

Mud Lake Lean-to was rebuilt in 1984 to replace one burned a few years previously, so it is one of the newest in the southern Adirondacks.

The trail crosses Mud Lake's vly on another plank bridge almost immediately after the lean-to. It follows along the lakeshore until at 4.0 mi. it turns away from Mud Lake, now heading ESE. At 4.6 mi. a section of trail covered with exposed roots is tricky to navigate, and an attractive little stream is encountered at 4.7 mi.

Climbing at 5.0 mi., the trail continues along the contour of a ridge and at 5.6 mi. crosses a larger creek. At 5.7 mi. the trail passes through a stand of large hemlocks, and then through a wildly overgrown area, swampy, with no bridges to assist the crossing. The trail here is muddy and lush with scrubby undergrowth. An old beaver lodge is seen here; the trail is obviously traversing the shoreline of a former beaver pond.

Climbing out of the boggy area, at 6.1 mi. the trail encounters another wet section, which is crossed at 6.2 mi. on a plank dual-split log bridge. Note the abundance of sphagnum moss. Farther along in this very wild area, asters, turtle heads and other wildflowers can be seen. Two small feeder streams leading into the bog are crossed and then the trail climbs out of the bog. A slight jog to the R occurs here. A steep descent commences at 6.6 mi. and at 6.7 mi., after the trail reaches the bottom of the hill and crosses a stream, Canary Pond appears on the R. From the top of the ridge the hiker can look down upon the emerald green waters of this lovely little pond, surrounded by evergreens, its shores dotted with large boulders.

Leaving the trail to explore Canary Pond, turn R where a faint path leads to a large campsite. The hiker can continue to the R along the shore another 300 yds. through the trees to the site of several glacial boulders which jut into the water, providing welcome access to deeper water for swimming and wonderful clear spaces to rest and picnic.

The trail continues on to Silver Lake through a large bog at the S end of Canary Pond. Here it becomes more difficult to follow due to several fallen trees which one must leave the trail to avoid. The blowdown also obscures the trail, causing the most careful trail-finder to wander into the wetter areas of the swamp. Mucking through in the right direction, however, will bring one to a series of half-submerged split log bridges spanning the next trail section. At 7.6 mi. the trail crosses a rocky area, then at 7.9 mi. passes through an open woods and up yet another moderate incline to follow the contours of the ridge. The trail then descends to cross a small stream at 8.0 mi. After a steady uphill climb it descends again, and at 8.9 mi. Silver Lake comes into sight. The lean-to is reached at 9.0 mi.

Silver Lake Lean-to faces away from the lake (1987), which is nice in the colder seasons when lake winds chill the camper but not in summer when a hiker may like the breeze and views of the water. However, DEC has plans to relocate the lean-to up the ridge, facing the lake, in the near future.

The waters of Silver Lake do, indeed, look silver when the wind and light are right. Whether or not one sees the lake as having a silver sparkle, it is very pretty with large rocks along the shore behind the lean-to that are handy for entering the water to swim or wade.

Distances: To Mud Lake Lean-to, 3.0 mi.; to beaver meadow, 5.7 mi.; to Canary Pond, 6.7 mi.; to tricky bog, 7.1 mi.; to Silver Lake Lean-to, 9.0 mi. (14.6 km.).

SILVER LAKE TO UPPER BENSON (N TO S)

Note: Mileages given are cumulative from Whitehouse; hikers cannot access Silver Lake except from the N at Whitehouse or S at Upper Benson.

Leaving Silver Lake lean-to and continuing around the lake, at 9.2 mi. the trail reaches the S end of the lake. Here a clear area along the shore is frequently used by campers, although it is too close to the lake for legal camping.

The trail now begins to climb moderately and turns SSW away from Silver Lake for approximately 0.2 mi., making several short meanders along the contour of a ridge. It then turns S again towards Benson. Along this section the trail is rather wild and rugged.

At 9.8 mi. Meco Lake is reached. The trail hugs the rough shoreline of Meco Lake, which although an attractive small body of water, is rapidly becoming a bog. Already the shores are filled with muck and swamp vegetation, but the trail has been marked along an elevated section of the shoreline.

Leaving Meco Lake, the hiker enters a pleasant, open wooded section, and at 10.2 mi. passes through a small wet area, then over a small stream, which can be rock-hopped, at 10.3 mi. The beautiful upper reaches of the West Branch of the Sacandaga River can be heard to the L before finally coming into sight at 10.5 mi. A series of small, enchanting waterfalls, each more lovely than the last, can be seen from the trail, which continues along the banks of the swift-flowing stream, several feet up the ridge above the water. At least three attractive rock-lined pools invite the summer hiker to wade or take a refreshing dip, although none appears more than a few feet deep.

At 10.7 mi. there is a benchmark on a large rock at the river's edge. Here the trail crosses the swift-running but shallow West Branch. There is no bridge, but during most of the year the hiker can easily rock-hop, even with a heavy pack.

Leaving the river, the trail immediately crosses a cleared area that at one time was used by logging crews and now, occasionally, by hunters as a camping area. The clearing is rapidly being reclaimed by the forest, but it still provides the hiker with sunshine and a riotous display of wild asters, goldenrod, and other seasonal field flowers. At 10.9 mi. a log corduroy spans a wet area and the trail enters a stand of cool, peaceful evergreens.

The trail traverses a series of small knolls and ridges, entering hardwoods again and passing through some of the most attractive woods found in the southern Adirondacks. Large maples, birches, beech and ash create splendid avenues of verdant shade. At approximately 2.4 mi. from the Silver Lake lean-to (18.0 mi. from NY 8 in Piseco; 11.6 mi. from Whitehouse) the waters of Rock Lake can be sighted occasionally through the trees to the R (S), but the trail keeps to the higher contour of a ridge. The descent to Rock Lake is made by turning R at 11.8 mi. where a trail sign points to Rock Lake and notes that it is 0.1 mi. (L for the hiker coming from S to N.)

A short trek down the ridge brings the hiker to the shore of lovely Rock Lake. Here are three large campsites, open and attractive—

evidently well used. The lake edges, however, are not sandy or rocky but rich in mucky mud, which makes wading or swimming an unattractive option.

Regaining the main trail, the hiker continues S, descending quickly to cross a tiny stream at the bottom of a col. At 12.8 mi. another small stream is crossed and then the trail makes a quick jog to the R. At 13.9 mi. it bears R again and downhill, crossing Goldmine Creek, where no bridge is available, at 14.0 mi. (There are ruins of a washed-out plank bridge.) There is a small camping area here. At 14.6 mi. difficult walking is encountered along a washed-out, rocky, downhill section of trail. There is a small creek flowing at the bottom of the ravine. Notice on the R at 14.7 mi. a huge dead tree with several large elongated holes chipped out of its trunk. These are the work of the pileated woodpecker.

After a short downhill section, the trail crosses a bridge over the fast-flowing North Branch of West Stony Creek at 14.9 mi. Just above the crossing is a series of small waterfalls.

After crossing this attractive watercourse, the trail immediately turns sharply L and follows West Stony Creek to the large open camping area at the end of a rutted dirt road at 15.3 mi. The road, which leads off to the R, brings the hiker at 16.5 mi. to the trailhead on Godfrey Road in Upper Benson. The trail register is reached at 7.3 mi. from the Silver Lake Lean-to.

Distances: Whitehouse to Meco Lake, 9.8 mi.; to Sacandaga crossing, 10.7 mi.; to Goldmine Creek crossing, 14.0 mi.; to North Branch of West Stony Creek crossing, 14.9 mi.; to Upper Benson DEC Trail Register, 16.5 mi. (26.6 km.).

Total distance: From NY 8 to Upper Benson, 23.1 mi. (37.2 km.)

Vly near East Canada Creek

Powley-Piseco Road

CANADA LAKE, CAROGA LAKE, AND POWLEY-PISECO ROAD SECTION

The western section of the southern region is more level than the other areas, and most trails are seldom used by the hiker. Criss-crossed by snowmobile trails that follow old logging and wagon roads, the area has some long and difficult treks—difficult to walk due to lowlands and swamps, difficult to follow due to lush plant growth. And yet, hiking here is a challenge precisely because it is so wild.

The larger lakes are surrounded for the most part by private land, and those that are in the Forest Preserve are often encircled by swampland. Nevertheless, they are lovely and isolated. Exploration will generally reveal one or two camping areas on higher ground.

The Powley-Piseco Road provides motorized access into some of the most remote trailheads. This largely unpaved road runs N-S between NY 10 and NY 29A for 19 miles. Many of the trails described as beginning along this road are snowmobile trails. While they would be fine for skiing, the road is not plowed in winter, and skiing the road *and* a trail would result in trips too long for the average cross-country skier to complete in one day.

Hikes recommended in this section are:

SHORT HIKES:

Kane Mt.—S. Trail—0.7 mi. A short but fairly vigorous hike up this popular mountain will be rewarded with views if the hiker also climbs the manned fire tower.

Nine Corner Lake—0.9 mi. Trek to a very pretty and popular blue-green lake with boulders along its shore that provide easy access for swimming.

MODERATE HIKES:

Big Alderbed—3.1 mi. An easy walk through beautiful hardwoods to a challenging stream crossing and, finally, a pretty little lake.

Stewart and Indian Lakes—2.3 mi. Hike an easy, mostly level trail to two charming small lakes.

HARDER HIKE:

Irving Pond, Bellows Lake and Holmes Lake Loop—8.3 mi. A wonderful circle trip with rolling terrain—an excellent ski trip, too.

BUSHWHACK

CLOCKMILL CORNERS TRAIL
TO CLOCKMILL POND

(To Rock Lake, Black Cat Lake and Kennel Pond, see below.)

An attractive old logging road has become a marked hiking and snowmobile trail leading into several ponds in this picturesque area.

The start of the trail is on the E (R if coming from the S) side of the Powley-Piseco Road, 14.7 mi. from the S end of the road where it begins on NY 29A outside of Stratford. A brown and yellow DEC sign at the trailhead says Clockmill Pond (no mileage listed); Kennel Pond, 5 mi.; Avery's Place, 6 mi.; Fulton County Snowmobile Trail—No Motorized Vehicles Except Snowmobiles.

The beginning of the trail traverses a small wet area, after which the path begins a slight ascent. It is relatively flat and travels through a mixed hardwood forest. At 0.1 mi. the trail bends L. On the L is a lush and pretty grassy vly. A rough snowmobile bridge spans part of this swampy section at 0.2 mi.

A small stream is crossed, and at 0.3 mi. the path leads across another wooden-plank snowmobile bridge that cuts across the vly in a SE direction. The trail is still relatively flat and pleasant walking through maple, beech, and other hardwoods. On a ridge at 0.4 mi. the trail continues through a stand of very mature trees, then descends to cross another bridge at 0.5 mi. This is a wood bridge in good condition, crossing a fast-flowing stream. After a swing to the L another small stream, at 0.6 mi., is diverted across the trail by an aluminum culvert. At 0.7 mi. the trail cuts to the R, and up a gentle grade. At 0.9 mi. a brief descent leads to a crossing on a snowmobile bridge at the bottom of a gully.

The trail crosses another stream before entering a large meadow filled with tall grasses at 1.1 mi. It crosses this meadow and forks to the L (E) to continue to Clockmill Pond on an unmarked but well-defined path. To the R is the marked snowmobile trail to Rock Lake, Black Cat Lake and Kennel Pond (see below).

Continuing to Clockmill Pond, proceed through a grove of hemlocks, then downhill at 1.2 mi. until at 1.3 mi. a junction offers a choice of L or R. To the L (E) there is an abundance of blowdown on the trail, but this fork soon takes the hiker to a view of a small back bay at 1.5 mi. However, no access to the lake is possible due to swamp and wild undergrowth.

An easier and more rewarding path to the shore of Clockmill Pond is the R fork, which continues another 0.2 mi. The path at times is very faint and difficult to follow in midsummer. Keep bearing L along and then over a small ridge; the S shore of the pond is soon accessible at 1.6 mi. There is a grassy campsite with room for at least one tent. Looking across this lovely little pond, it appears that there are additional camping spots, although the poor condition of the trail, and no trails that can be found around the pond in midsummer, mean the determined hiker will have to plan on bushwhacking to discover a suitable camping area.

Distances: To meadow junction, 1.1 mi.; to Clockmill Pond, 1.6 mi. (2.6 km.).

CLOCKMILL CORNERS TO KENNEL POND VIA ROCK LAKE

Take the Clockmill Corners Trail to the meadow and junction at 1.1 mi. The hiker who wishes to proceed to Rock Lake, Black Cat Lake and/or Kennel Pond, should take the marked snowmobile trail to the R. Proceed downhill and across a large area of blowdown at 1.15 mi. At 1.2 mi. cross a creek on a wooden snowmobile bridge. The trail follows the contours of a ridge for a short distance until at 1.4 mi. it passes on the L an unnamed pond surrounded by an impenetrable swamp. At 1.45 mi. a little creek flows into the pond, and then another small stream comes from the R to gurgle across the trail. After a short but steep uphill section, the trail swings away from the lake. At 1.5 mi. a wooden bridge with beautiful side rails spans a large brook.

Rock Lake comes into view between the trees and at 1.8 mi. can be seen clearly on the L. The trail does not go directly along the shore but rather keeps to the higher ground of a ridge.

(The faint trace of the old path to Black Cat Lake is 10 to 15 ft. up a small ridge after a stream is crossed directly opposite Rock Pond— there is a blaze on a tree. Go to the R if you are coming from Clockmill Corners. This bushwhack proceeds WSW. See below.)

At 2.0 mi. an enormous hemlock has been cleared from the trail. Notice the exceptionally mature specimens of large paper birch on both sides of the trail. At 2.3 mi. the trail continues S, descending sharply to a lower section of the ridge. At 2.6 mi. another, newer snowmobile bridge is laid across another boggy area. At this point the trail becomes indistinct and most difficult to discern. It appears that a new trail was once partially cleared along the side of the ridge, probably to avoid the lower wet areas. At 2.8 mi. another stream is crossed; the trail is rocky and wildly overgrown here, thanks to erosion during periods of heavy rain.

A junction at 3.0 mi. also marks the W end of Kennel Pond (also known as Avery's Lake). There is a snowmobile trail to the N, Wagnor's Loop. Do not try to hike this trail as it is so overgrown it is impossible to find after the first half-mile. The determined hiker will need a map and compass and must be prepared to walk through swamps.

The main trail continues R and across another wooden snowmobile bridge, heading toward Arietta. It crosses another creek at 3.9 mi. and has left the vly on the L. Kennel Pond comes into view at 4.0 mi. The hiker is now on private property although the trail continues along the lake, then across a short ridge, to reach a junction with an old road at 4.5 mi. that appears to be infrequently walked. Continue along the road to reach the private lands along NY 10, where hikers could spot a car, after asking permission, of course. Otherwise, the trek to return to Powley-Piseco Road is in excess of 9.0 mi., roundtrip.

Distances: Powley-Piseco Road to Rock Lake, 1.9 mi.; to junction, 3.0 mi.; to Kennel Pond, 4.0 mi. (6.5 km.).

BLACK CAT LAKE

BUSHWHACK

Black Cat Lake—an intriguing name belonging to a pretty little body of water that is slowly degenerating into a swamp. Although there is supposed to have been, years ago, a primitive road to this picturesque body of water, all outward signs have been obliterated by the encroaching forest. Using a map and compass, however, the intrepid hiker can, with careful observation, bushwhack to this lake. The trip is challenging and not long, but the hiker must pay close attention to landmarks and the map and compass. (See above, Clockmill Corners Trail to Kennel Pond via Rock Lake, for trail description to Rock Lake.)

To find the cutoff point, follow the Clockmill Pond trail 1.9 mi. to where it crosses a medium-sized stream opposite Rock Lake, then continues up a hill to the top of a ridge. A small beech tree on the L has a blaze cut into its trunk at eye level. Here a careful perusal to the R of the trail will disclose a faint path heading WSW. This very faint path peters out rather quickly, but the determined hiker should continue W through the draw and then jog a bit to the R. Occasional old blazes will be found on trees. Continue on this W compass bearing and a small marshy area will appear on the L.

Proceed through the draw, bearing somewhat R and upward to get to the top of a ridge. Then descend the ridge through the col until a dry stream bed is encountered. Follow this rock-strewn, washed-out stream bed until the lake comes into sight. No trail is evident in midsummer; thus the old wagon road has, for all practical purposes, reverted back to the forest. Witch hobble and other shrubs and large ferns are found in abundance.

Black Cat Lake should be sighted after 40 to 45 minutes of tedious bushwhacking. The lake is lovely but swampy and boggy around its entire shoreline. The hiker can, however, carefully walk to the edge of the water on exposed mud flats and grass tufts. It is approximately 3 miles (one way) to Black Cat Lake from the Powley-Piseco Road trailhead.

Distances: To cutoff from Clockmill Corners Trail, 1.9 mi.; to Black Cat Lake (approximate) 3.0 mi. (4.9 km.).

BIG ALDERBED

Big Alderbed is an attractive small lake that was made much larger at one time by the addition of a dam to accommodate the needs of the logging industry in the early 1900s. Since then most of the dam has eroded and flooded away, although periodically it is partially rebuilt by beavers. The old road, now a marked snowmobile trail, is a pleasant day's round trip walk for the average hiker.

To reach the start of the trail, take the Powley-Piseco Road N for approximately 11.1 mi. to a bridge with iron railings that look like old bed headboards. It spans the West Branch of East Canada Creek. Park on the S side of the bridge where there is plenty of room on both road shoulders.

The trail begins on the L (W) side of the road, a bit S of the iron-railed bridge. This former logging road is generally flat and passes through an attractive forest of hardwoods mixed with scattered stands of evergreens.

There is a camping area just off the road through which the trail passes to enter a small thicket of hemlocks. A series of railroad ties has been laid over a wet area at 0.1 mi. At 0.2 mi. there is a slight jog L. Walking is pleasant due to the absence of boulders and blowdown; the terrain is flat for the most part. The trail reaches a clearing at 0.3 mi. and soon crosses a brook.

A short uphill section traverses the side of a ridge, still following the old roadbed, and at 0.4 mi. reaches the crest of the ridge. The trail crosses a tiny stream that flows in from the L at 0.7 mi. A mucky area at 0.8 mi. can be avoided by walking to the L or R. The trail now bends sharply R and descends, crossing another wet area on an old log corduroy.

Still traveling W, the trail crosses a small brook at 0.9 mi. and then begins a moderate climb out of its gully. A larger stream can be rock-hopped at 1.0 mi. The forest is open; several very large trees obviously escaped the axes of the lumberjacks, perhaps because they shaded their road. At 1.3 mi. the trail passes through a boggy area strewn with big rocks and crosses yet another small stream at 1.4 mi. Snowmobile signs point the way through a grove of birch and beech trees.

At 1.7 mi. there is a quick jog L and the trail begins climbing moderately, reaching the crest of the ridge at 1.9 mi. The trail then continues downhill to cross a wet area at 2.1 mi. and jog R around a large blowdown. A larger stream is reached at 2.2 mi. It can be crossed to the L where a huge moss-covered boulder is located.

After crossing this stream, the path leads up a ridge to the R. In the vicinity of 2.3 mi. the trail becomes wildly overgrown in midsummer although it is still faintly discernible. At 2.4 mi. a swing R occurs, then a slight descent. At 2.6 mi. another brook is crossed, followed by a steeper section.

At 2.7 mi. the trail reaches the swift-flowing outlet of Big Alderbed. This is an exciting watercourse whose crossing can be dicey during periods of high water. The hiker should scout carefully for a safe crossing. Boulders (or perhaps a log) can almost always be found downstream, unless the water is very high. There is also an old rusted cable about 50 yds. downstream that has been used in the past for crossing. However, it no longer appears to be safe. Hikers may want to bushwhack upstream to the dam across the outlet of Big Alderbed, approximately three-tenths of a mile, and attempt to cross there. One of the exciting aspects of this hike is solving the dilemma of crossing the stream, although in midsummer and dry times it is not a big problem.

After crossing the stream, the trail follows the creek due W until a feeder stream is encountered at 2.9 mi. Here the trail swings away from the water and up a knoll through a rocky area marked sporadically by snowmobile signs. The path again becomes indistinct, but with care it can still be followed.

At 3.1 mi. the trail reaches Big Alderbed Lake. A small, grass-covered camping area graces the shore at the end of the trail and is very pleasant. Note the remains of the wood and rock dam to the L, about 50 yds. from the camping area where the outlet begins. Proceed R, following the fishermen's path around the NE shore. Boulders offer attractive places to eat lunch and meditate on the quiet loveliness of this wild little lake, parts of which are all too quickly changing into swampland. The entire N end is now a marsh, and the relative absence of trees along the shore attests to the recent loss of several feet of water when the old dam eroded. Small mountains in the near distance contribute to this small lake's overall scenic attractiveness.

Distances: To large stream to rock-hop, 1.0 mi.; to stream with large mossy boulder, 2.1 mi.; to outlet crossing, 2.7 mi.; to Big Alderbed, 3.1 mi. (5.0 km.).

MECO LAKE

This is a walk on the wild side, recommended for anyone curious to see what lumbering does to a forest. In the right season, numerous wild berries can be picked enroute.

The trail begins off the Powley-Piseco Road across from Mud Pond, 4.5 mi. from the iron bridge over East Canada Creek. A snowmobile trail, it has no sign other than the prominent disks marking the path.

The trail begins traveling due N on the W side of the Powley-Piseco Road. For the first 0.1 mi. it climbs a small incline. There are numerous large hardwood trees, especially large yellow birches. Although the trail is discernible and adequately marked with the disks and old blazes, it is not well defined or recently improved. The top of a ridge is reached at 0.2 mi. The forest is open and attractive.

Still heading N, at 0.3 mi. the trail crosses a small brook which has no bridge, and continues up a gentle grade. After a quick jog to the R, note the remains of old logs underfoot. Someone has strategically placed wooden pallets across wet sections of the trail. The trail traverses a swampy area at 0.4 mi. and crosses a stream at 0.5 mi.; again, there is no bridge.

Continuing up a gentle grade, the trail passes a huge maple tree at 0.6 mi. The crest of this ridge is reached at 0.7 mi. The trail then descends slightly and bends a bit to the R. Mature beech and birch trees, but no evergreens, are encountered along this section.

The trail passes through a rough, rocky area at 1.0 mi. The undergrowth becomes lush with ferns and nettles and crosses a soggy, swampy area where it becomes difficult to follow. On the other side of this bog the trail is easily found again, after which it begins a gentle descent (although this can be classified as a flat trail for most of its length).

A small stream with a rustic makeshift bridge is crossed at 1.2 mi.

At 1.25 mi. a tree bears a sign indicating that motorized vehicles are prohibited beyond this point; this is the boundary line between private and state land. Within 50 ft. the trail jogs L, then continues down a gentle descent. A logging road is reached at 1.4 mi. and berry bushes begin. This is a seemingly endless blackberry and raspberry patch with treacherous footing—depressions and rocks one cannot see while walking through the vines and leaves. The trail crosses a small stream at 1.5 mi.; the prickly berry bushes continue as far as the eye can see. The direction of travel is NW. There is a big log culvert at 1.7 mi. on the R. There are no snowmobile disks or trail markers in this area. At 1.8 mi. is another stream, difficult to cross due to deep pits filled with water and slippery old logs.

At 1.9 mi. Meco Lake can be seen through the trees on the L. To reach the lakeshore, the hiker must leave the old logging road and descend about 150 yds. through the brush to the boggy shore. Meco Lake is small and picturesque, but it has a swampy shoreline and the water is out of reach for the hiker.

Although the old logging trail continues W, it is very difficult to walk due to the berry bushes and the numerous huge ruts, and it is filled with water and debris left by the logging operations in the late 1970s. It will be years before the forest returns and heals the scars.

Distances: To state land boundary, 1.25 mi.; to Meco Lake, 2.0 mi. (3.2 km.).

SAND LAKE

A deep, wild, and remote lake, this is a very short and an easy trip to make carrying a canoe to do further explorations. At the end of the trail on the shore is a lovely clearing with extremely pretty views across the lake.

The trail begins on the R (E) side of Powley-Piseco Road, 17 mi. from the S end. It immediately passes through two camping clearings and begins to descend. At 0.1 mi. there is a jog to the R; then a sharp L to traverse a large wet, mucky section at 0.3 mi. This boggy area cannot be avoided easily L or R, and the hiker must pick a way through and over, using grass tufts and skinny branches and roots as stepping areas, sometimes getting a wet and muddy boot.

After this swampy area, the trail crosses a small stream on a makeshift log bridge, and begins to climb a small grade. At the top of this knoll Sand Lake can be seen through the trees. A brief descent through a smaller wet area can be avoided by swinging L. At 0.5 mi. the path ends in a large grassy clearing on the W shore of Sand Lake.

The outlet is to the R of the campsite where evidence of sporadic beaver activity exists in the form of washed-out dams and debris. Sand Lake, long rather than wide, curves out of sight. Big, beautiful rocks come down to the shore in several places. An irregular shoreline with many little bays makes this an interesting lake to explore by canoe. Sand Lake is wild and much of the shoreline is impenetrable spruce and tangled underbrush. One loon was seen during the summer of 1986 and a pair may be nesting there.

Distances: To unavoidable boggy area, 0.3 mi.; to Sand Lake, 0.5 mi. (0.8 km.).

SHERIFF LAKE

Buildings once dotted the shore of Sheriff Lake, but now nothing is left but the stone foundations and riotous flowers gone wild from the gardens of the former inhabitants.

Because of logging operations in much of the surrounding forests in recent years, the former trails into this and Jones and Indigo lakes are no longer viable. The only reasonable approach to Sheriff Lake at present is from the N off NY 8.

Access to the trail is on the S side of NY 8 two miles W of the junction of NY 8 and the Northern Shore Road around Piseco Lake.

The trailhead is unmarked and difficult to spot from the road. It is now marked by a hole in the trees. Look carefully for a stretch of old macadam road now overgrown and almost hidden on the S side of NY 8. There is plenty of space for parking here.

The sharp-eyed hiker will see the ruins of a barrier, consisting of two rusted iron posts hidden in the trees, just off the macadam stretch. The trail is the remains of an old road, very overgrown.

The hiker immediately begins to descend a small grade, going S, crossing a tiny stream at 0.1 mi. at the bottom of the hill. A wild, swampy meadow off to the L can be seen through the trees, although it is hidden from the road.

At 0.3 mi. the trail becomes much better defined and not so overgrown. The hiker wearing shorts must avoid lots of nettles. The forest is young, as it was logged in the last 10 or 15 years and is now recovering. The trees are hardwoods, mostly sugar maples, beech, and ash. The old road is fairly flat and straight with a great deal of blowdown. At 0.4 mi. it makes a slight bend to the R, and a medium-sized creek flows on the L about 50 yds. from the path. At 0.45 mi. this creek is crossed on an ancient, broken and hazardous wood bridge with several gaping holes in it.

Ascending a small rise at 0.5 mi., the trail reaches a cleared area at 0.6 mi., which is the intersection of a snowmoblie trail that runs E and W. A rough sign says Bearpath Inn and points W (see below).

Deep ruts in the path indicate heavy ATV activity in this area. There are also many summer field flowers. The main trail continues in a general S direction (straight ahead). At 0.7 mi. a stream runs under a culvert. The remains of an old building can be explored on the R. Many logging roads criss-cross this area, but the hiker should continue walking S along the old road.

At 0.9 mi. Sheriff Lake comes into view as the road tops a small hill. Here an old farm once flourished, and there still are ruins of at least three buildings to the L and R of the trail. Two enormous, ancient sugar maples are still standing to the L. Spring and summer will find the hillside decorated by the hardy ancestors of cultivated flowers still sending forth shoots of magnificent magenta and violet, pink and yellow, scattered among the less showy wildflowers.

Descending to the shore of Sheriff Lake, which is reached at 1.1 mi., one finds a very wet walk to the edge of the water. Yet it is an attractive little lake, home to at least one agitated loon when this writer visited it in the wet summer of 1986.

The hiker may wish to explore several of the wide logging roads left by those who did extensive logging throughout this area in the 1970s. These wide roads are often attractive to walk, leading one through large sections of wildflowers and mossy, damp areas with interesting plants like scouring rushes—typical of a recovering natural area. However, with the exception of the main logging road to the E, they go nowhere. Already the forest is growing back, although slowly. It appears as though much of the lumbering was clear-cutting, as there are no trees of any significant size left.

Exploration of the logging roads will clearly show the main E corridor, which goes for 2.0 mi. and leads the exploring hiker to NY 8 and the intersection of the Northern Shore Road around Piseco Lake. The logged lands are unposted from the interior but are posted as private at this entrance on NY 8.

Distances: To intersection of Bearpath Inn Trail, 0.6 mi.; to shore of Sheriff Lake, 1.1 mi. (1.8 km.).

BEARPATH INN TRAIL TO SHERIFF LAKE

A short, relatively flat walk through open hardwoods with some marshy sections to negotiate, this is, nevertheless, a pleasant walk to a pretty lake with old ruins to explore.

The trail begins one-quarter mile east of Alderbrook Road on the S side of NY 8, heading S. Marked as a snowmobile trail, the path proceeds through a level, open woods with prolific fern growth. At 0.2 mi. the trail passes through a brief marshy area and then crosses a plank snowmobile bridge. A second swampy area is reached shortly after the bridge. Here several mature trees have been cut, for some mysterious reason, 5 and 6 ft. from the ground, then left lying at the side of the trail—perhaps illegally cut in winter and never removed? At 0.3 mi. the trail turns L, then R again to head SE. At 0.7 mi. the trail traverses a large wet section which, in midsummer, contains a heavy growth of large nettle plants unpleasant to walk through, especially for the hiker wearing shorts.

For the next three-quarters of a mile the trail traverses flat open woodlands, in a generally E direction, then begins a barely perceptible descent. At 1.6 mi. the trail makes a sharp turn L and begins to descend moderately. The woods are very open and pleasant, predominantly hardwoods with very few evergreens. At 2.0 mi. the junction of an old road is reached. Turn R and continue an additional 0.5 mi. (2.5 mi.) to Sheriff Lake. (See Sheriff Lake description above.)

Distances: To junction of old road to Sheriff Lake, 2.0 mi.; to Sheriff Lake, 2.5 mi. (4.1 km.).

STEWART AND INDIAN LAKES

This hike is a moderate, mostly level walk to two interesting and charming destinations. Indian Lake is by far the jewel of the two, yet Stewart has its own mystery and peace.

To reach the trailhead, drive on NY 10 to the Canada Lake-Green Lake area and turn N onto Green Lake Road, which follows the W shore of Green Lake. Travel 0.6 mi. to a L fork—the shore road continues and makes a sharp R. Take the L onto a little used dirt road extension and go about 200 yds. to a parking turnout on the R. To the L is the E trailhead up Kane Mt. Park here, because the road shortly becomes very rough and then, immediately after passing tiny Fish Hatchery Pond, is barred by a chain. It continues to Otter Lake, which is private. However, before Fish Hatchery Pond is reached, the trail can be seen on the R, marked with a DEC trail sign that says: Stewart Lake 1.25 mi.; Indian Lake 2.0 mi. The trail is also marked with yellow and black cross-country ski trail markers.

A very short walk, less than one-tenth of a mile up the road past the trailhead, will bring the hiker to the old concrete dam at the outlet of Fish Hatchery Pond. Here one might cross the dam and continue up the small hill to join the trail at the top, but hikers who prefer to stay on the marked trail should follow the trail at the sign. The trail immediately passes through a hemlock grove and across a sturdy plank bridge spanning the outlet of Fish Hatchery Pond. It then climbs the short ridge that overlooks the tiny pond, reaching the top at 0.1 mi.

The trail traverses the shore on top of the ridge for a short distance. It is well defined, traveling through a mixed hardwood and hemlock forest. Wildflowers—red trilliums, bellworts, canada lilies, and colorful violets—abound in spring. The general direction is E. At 0.2 mi. the trail enters an avenue of hemlocks. The trail twists and turns until at 0.3 mi. it leaves Fish Hatchery Pond behind. Climbing

Sheriff Lake Chimney

moderately, it enters more open hardwoods, with a blanket of witch hobble growing beneath the young beech and ash trees.

A tiny brook is crossed by rock-hopping at 0.4 mi., and the trail continues uphill at a moderate pitch. At the top of a ridge a large downed beech tree provides a resting place. After a jog R at 0.6 mi., the trail soon passes two huge glacial erratics which are most unusual. They are sedimentary and striped in subtle colors of yellow, pink and gray.

A small wet area is encountered at 0.7 mi., after which the trail begins to climb more steeply. At 0.8 mi. the trail makes a slight jog L and then follows the contours of a ridge at 0.9 mi. A steady uphill climb commences at 1.1 mi. in a NE direction to top a ridge at 1.2 mi.

The descent to Stewart Lake, which can now be sighted through the trees, begins at 1.3 mi. Because the shoreline is 90 percent marshland, the trail does not go close to the lake but keeps to higher ground. The trail crosses a large wet section that is an arm of the shoreline bog at 1.5 mi.

Hikers who wish to descend to the lake should watch for a hemlock stand at 1.6 mi. on the L and bushwhack through it on the high ground, which here continues to the shore, providing minimal access to the water. Stewart Lake is small but attractive and, due to its protected shores, rather pristine.

The trail continues to hug the high ground to the E and shortly turns NE towards Indian Lake, veering away from Stewart. It crosses a wet area with a small brook running through it at 1.8 mi. and continues through a level section. The woods are very open and the trail is smooth and easy underfoot, beginning a downhill section at 2.0 mi. After a jog R, at 2.1 mi. Indian Lake comes into view. The trail descends and crosses a little brook to reach the lakeshore.

A path to the L along the shore leads another 0.2 mi. to a huge rock that juts out into the lake. This enormous and attractive rock contains small pockets of garnet interspersed with feldspar, an interesting and attractive combination. The rock is a fine observation and/or picnic spot, high and surrounded by hemlock and spruce. The shores of Indian Lake are mostly lined with swampy, tangled, low brush, but there are a few rocks here and there, and behind the marshy areas are attractive spruce and hemlock thickets that help create a peaceful and picturesque destination.

Distances: To descent to Stewart Lake, 1.3 mi.; to Indian Lake shore, 2.1 mi.; to huge garnet rock, 2.3 mi. (3.7 km.).

KANE MT. FROM THE EAST

One of three trails up Kane Mt. (see below), the trail from the E is marked with DEC trail markers and can be reached by turning N on Green Lake Road and driving 0.6 mi. to the end of the lake, where there is a fork L. The lake road continues sharply to the R. Take the L, which is a less used dirt road, and within 200 yds. there is a parking area on the R, with the marked trail to Kane Mt. on the L. The brown and yellow DEC sign says Kane Mt. Observatory 0.5 mi., although the actual distance is 0.9 mi.

The trail begins to climb immediately through a broad avenue of mature hardwoods. At 0.1 mi. it bends R, and at 0.2 mi. it continues through a series of small jogs L and R until at 0.6 mi. it straightens out. The trail is moderately steep and well used, although trail markers seem to be absent. There are a number of twists and turns in this old jeep road. As the summit is approached the trail becomes level and passes through a cleared area where numerous berry bushes appear to be trying to gain a permanent foothold. The last several feet are through a grassy clearing, then past the observer's cabin. The trail turns R to the fire tower area.

Distances: To summit of Kane Mt., 0.9 mi. (1.5 km.).

KANE MT. VIA THE SOUTH TRAIL

A hike to the summit of Kane Mt. is a short walk to a manned fire tower, which offers several additional areas to explore. There is an observer's cabin and grassy picnic area on top, although no views are available unless the hiker climbs the tower. From the summit, trails lead down the E side and across the ridge and down the N slope, then W to Pine Lake Campground. (See above and below.)

To reach the trailhead on the S side, turn onto Schoolhouse Road from NY 10. The road is located on the N (R) side, approximately 0.4 mi. from Green Lake Road, which is also on the R immediately after passing Green Lake. About 150 yds. up this dirt road is the start of the marked trail on the R. A parking area carved into the shoulder of the road is large enough for two or three cars.

The trail begins to climb immediately at a moderately steep grade. At 0.2 mi. it is rocky and well used, but wide and clear. The forest is open and is composed of a preponderance of sugar maples as well as other hardwoods such as ash, yellow birch and beech.

At 0.3 mi. the climb becomes steeper, with sections of loose earth and stone underfoot. A large tree trunk is lying at the side of the trail, and a maple tree is growing in the center at 0.4 mi. At 0.5 mi. a few hemlocks come into view—their sporadic dark green against the background of red and yellow maples makes a pretty scene in the fall.

At 0.6 mi. the tower comes into view. As the hiker approaches the tower, the trail levels and the observer's cabin appears on the R about 150 yds. off the trail. The tower is still used, and an observer is in residence throughout the summer months. Views can be had only from the tower; on a good day, one can see S as far as the Catskills and N to the High Peaks, while in the near distance Pine Lake (NW) and West Canada Lake (S) are a delight to the eye.

Hikers wishing to make a circle trip and return to their cars via Green Lake and NY 10 may take the trail to the R which begins just past the cabin and through a clearing heading due E. The total round trip distance is 1.5 mi.

Distance: To summit of Kane Mt, 0.7 mi. (1.1 km.).

KANE MT. FROM PINE LAKE CAMPGROUND

A third route up Kane Mt. is through Pine Lake Campground. Part of this trail is an old road marked as a cross-country ski trail. It circles the foot of the mountain to arrive at the E trail up Kane Mt. (see above), then continues on to intersect the dirt road along the shore of Little Green Lake.

To reach the trailhead at Pine Lake Campground, take NY 10 to the junction of 10 and NY 29A and turn where the sign indicates Pine Lake Paradise Campsite. Drive to the entrance of the campground and the general store. Hikers and skiers are permitted to park here and proceed on foot (or skis) into the campground itself. Follow the signs to Chipmunk Cove, then Wilderness Way, at the end of which the trail begins near campsite W7.

The trail begins climbing through a rocky ravine and at 0.2 mi. leaves the ravine to climb a small ridge. Here the trail is very attractive, passing through an open forest of mature hardwoods. At 0.6 mi. it reaches the top of the ridge.

The easy-to-follow path bends to the L at 1.0 mi. and begins a downhill section. The hiker who wishes to climb Kane Mt. must look carefully here for the path to the R to begin the climb. The path is marked by a medium-sized old tree with red paint and indistinct carvings on its trunk. This is the beginning of a trail up Kane Mt., which is marked by yellow blazes much of the way.

(Hikers who choose to follow the old road and delay or forego a walk to the summit will circle around the foot of the mountain, following the contours of a long ridge. The path continues along a moderate descent and at 1.6 mi. reaches Fish Hatchery Pond and the dirt road extension of Green Lake Road on the E side. To the N (L) this rocky road shortly is blocked by a chain barrier and sign that says "No Trespassing," prohibiting access to Otter Lake. Take the S or R turn past the old cement dam a quarter-mile to the trailhead on the E that leads back up Kane Mt., or continue to Green Lake Road another one-eighth of a mile.)

After making the R to climb Kane Mt. the trail reaches the top of the large ridge that comprises the N approach to the summit at 1.3 mi. The trail traverses the ridge, up and down a col, until at 1.6 mi. it passes a section where a view is available in winter but not in summer because of the leaves on the trees.

The trail passes between two enormous glacial erratics at 1.7 mi. They are interesting because they seem so out of place, and attractive because they are multicolored. At 1.8 mi. the trail bears to the L and soon the summit is reached at 2.0 mi.

Distances: To S (R) turn marked with red-paint blazed tree, 1.0 mi.; to summit of Kane Mt., 2.0 mi. (3.2 km.); to Fish Hatchery Pond via old road, 1.6 mi. (2.6 km.).

NINE CORNER LAKE

An old road forms the trailbed to this extremely attractive little lake that is only 0.9 mi. from NY 29A, providing numerous campers with an interesting destination without much work. Heavily used in the summer, Nine Corner Lake is one of the jewels of the southern Adirondacks. Unfortunately, its sparkling quality is dulled by the behavior of hikers and campers who leave behind their piles of trash. Nevertheless, it is worth the short hike to savor the visual delights of a blue lake surrounded by enormous boulders and dark green pines.

The trail begins at the parking turn-off on NY 29A immediately after it splits off from NY 10 in the hamlet of Pine Lake. Parking is available on both sides of the highway, but the trail to Nine Corner Lake begins on the N (R) side at a brown and yellow DEC sign. A barrier is encountered as the trail leaves the parking area, with a trail register immediately thereafter. Motorized vehicles are prohibited according to a posted sign.

The trail is very well used, broad and smooth. It begins to climb immediately, although moderately, becoming a bit rocky at 0.2 mi. At 0.4 mi. an attractive stream on the L is seen about 100 yds. off the trail. At 0.5 mi. the trail flattens out, and at 0.6 mi. a sturdy plank snowmobile bridge crosses the swift-flowing outlet stream. To the R is a series of small waterfalls.

The trail continues climbing slightly, reaching a fork at 0.85 mi. Turn R for Nine Corner Lake. Note that this E (R) fork shows signs of being the more used of the two trails.

The lovely blue lake is reached at 0.9 mi. A rocky dam is on the E (R) side here at the outlet; a path leads across it and continues along the opposite side of the lake to clear areas which are frequently used for camping. The S end is strewn with large boulders that lead down into the water and create excellent access steps for the swimmer. A well-used camping area is a few yds. to the L on the S shore.

Distances: To bridge over outlet stream, 0.5 mi.; to Nine Corner Lake, 0.9 mi. (1.5 km.).

GLASGOW MILLS AND HILLABRANDT VLY

The trip to Glasgow Mills and Hillabrandt Vly is a moderate walk along an old woods road to the historic site of an old mill and then on to a picturesque vly. To reach the trailhead, heading N on NY 10, turn L onto Glasgow Mills Road, 1.0 mi. N of the junction of NY 10 and 10A. Proceed for 1.0 mi. where a parking and turn-around area is located at the end of the drivable section. Here there is a DEC sign which says: Glasgow Mills, 1.25 mi.; Hillabrandt Vly 3.0 mi.; County Road 119, 5.8 mi.; Snowmobile trail #4.

The trail is a continuation of the road and appears to be heavily used by ATVs. It passes through a predominantly hardwood forest with a few medium-sized hemlocks. The large creek on the R is Glasgow Creek, which is crossed at 0.2 mi. on a partially destroyed board bridge.

The trail continues along the road, which is rutted and muddy, and begins a moderate climb up the side of a ridge at 0.5 mi. At 0.6 mi. a cut-off goes to the R, but the marked snowmobile trail continues straight ahead.

At 1.0 mi. the trail descends a small hill and enters an area of hemlock and beech trees. The trail is very wet in sections, but these can generally be avoided to the R or L. It curves L and at 1.1 mi. swift-flowing Glasgow Creek comes into view again. There is another muddy section at 1.2 mi. and then the trail continues up a small hill. A small stand of white pines tops the hill at 1.3 mi.; the clearing known as Glasgow Mills lies beyond. Descending the knoll, the trail passes by what remains of the old dam, which in days past created a small lake to power a mill.

A side trail turns L around the old pond and crosses an open area that shows frequent use by ATV campers and picnickers. Depending upon the time of year and the local beaver population, there may or may not be a pond worthy of the name. There are abundant field

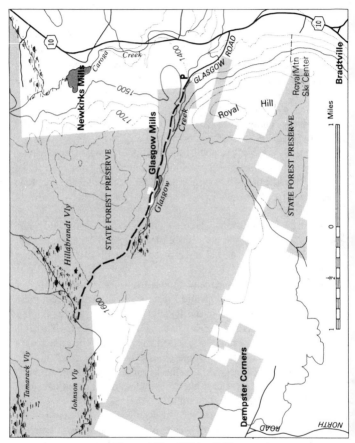

Glasgow Mills to Hillabrandt Vly

flowers in season, and a careful perusal of the area will reveal evidence of deer and coyote. Several clear paths lead to the water. This is a pleasant area to rest and have lunch or a trail snack. A second trail enters from the R, but the main trail continues straight ahead, circling the R (N) side of the old pond.

A big, muddy water hole must be circumvented at 1.5 mi. as the trail continues W. At least two cellar holes of old houses are passed at 1.6 mi. The trail turns R and crosses a swampy area, then begins a moderate uphill section, still through a predominantly hardwood forest.

At 2.2 mi. a creek running down the trail creates a very wet, if shallow, section, after which the soggy trail continues over another knoll. This begins a series of small undulations. At 2.3 mi. hemlocks are more in evidence; at 2.7 mi. they are especially attractive. At 2.9 mi. the trail passes through a thicket of balsam trees—a fragrant reward of a woods walk.

The trail reaches Hillabrandt Vly at 3.3 mi. and continues around it to the L, but the hiker should stop to enjoy the picturesque clearing to the R along the shore of a recently created pond. Beaver have been busy restoring the water level in the vly. Their dam is approximately 3 ft. high and has successfully, although no doubt temporarily, recreated a pond. Here, along the edge of the vly bordering the water, is a small stand of large, very beautiful white pines.

Distances: To Glasgow Mills clearing and pond, 1.4 mi.; to Hillabrandt Vly, 3.3 mi. (5.3 km.).

THIRD LAKE FROM NY 10

This trail provides access to many additional old roads and snowmobile trails. It is a pleasant, if sometimes wet, easy walk through level terrain. Third Lake has mostly swampy shores, but there is at least one nice campsite.

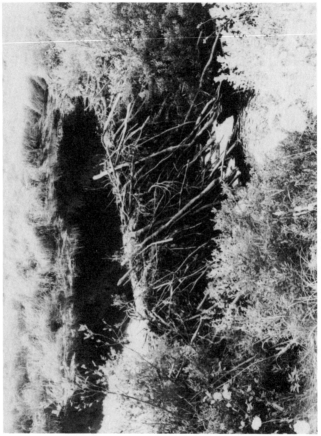

Arietta Beaver Dam

The trail begins in Arietta, off NY 10 to the E (L), a quarter of a mile S of the Arietta Hotel. The brown and yellow DEC trail sign is readily seen from the road. Park along the shoulder of NY 10.

Immediately at the bottom of the embankment of the road, the trail is very likely to be quite wet and mucky for at least the first 500 yds. At 0.2 mi. a second wet area must be crossed. This first 0.3 mi. has been recently established to avoid private land. At 0.3 mi. the trail makes a sharp L to join an old logging road, which used to be the trailhead leading back to the road. A sign on the R warns not to trespass on the private land.

The trail is overgrown but a definite path heading W, passing through a mixed forest including balsam and apple trees. After a bend to the L and another wet area at 0.4 mi. the trail curves to the R, still going through a thicket of aromatic balsam trees.

Although lush with plant life, this section is easy, pleasant walking in midsummer. At 0.5 mi. the trail passes through mixed hardwoods. There is a jog R at 0.6 mi., and the trail begins climbing a rise at 0.7 mi. This is the NW shoulder of Rooster Hill.

The trail levels again at 0.8 mi. and makes a turn to the L, then begins to descend at 0.9 mi. Soon the trail becomes rocky and uneven, and at 1.0 mi. a mucky section must be crossed. At 1.1 mi. a junction is reached. Here a DEC sign points R to Good Luck Lake, Avery's Place and Piseco, and L to West Stoner Lake.

Continue straight ahead, WSW towards Pleasant Lake and NY 29A, which the sign confirms. At 1.1 mi. the trail bends L and goes up a small incline. At 1.2 mi. it jogs to the R and then crests the small ridge at 1.3 mi. Climbing a bit more to top another small ridge on the N face of West Lake Mt. at 1.4 mi., the trail then descends moderately to cross a small stream. It soon bends slightly L at 1.5 mi. The trail goes L or R through a wet spot at 1.7 mi., and at 1.8 mi. passes through more open hardwood forest, heading W.

At 1.9 mi. a clearing with large, attractive rocks scattered about is traversed. The trail passes through very lovely rocky terrain at 2.0 mi. and then encounters a swampy area. It crosses a major creek at 2.4 mi. and several small wet areas until at 2.7 mi. Third Lake can be seen through the trees. The lake has a predominantly swampy shoreline. The trail winds along the E shore, traveling in a SSW direction. A camping area is reached at 2.8 mi. on higher ground on the shore of the lake.

Third Lake is attractive and seldom visited, probably because of the limited access to its waters due to the boggy shore line.

Distances: To junction of snowmobile trail to Stoner Lake and Good Luck Lake, 1.0 mi.; to clearing, 1.9 mi.; to Third Lake, 2.7 mi. (4.4 km.).

DRY AND DEXTER LAKES

BUSHWHACK TO SPECTACLE

The hike to Dry and Dexter lakes is an easy and attractive walk along an old road through open forests. The terrain is relatively flat, with moderate ups and downs which make the area most agreeable for cross-country skiing as well as hiking.

Dexter and Dry lakes are small and relatively isolated, but accessible to the hiker who wants an easy day's walk. For the more adventuresome, this walk can be combined with a bushwhack to Spectacle Lake for a circular return. Although the trail as far as Dexter Lake is well defined and marked as a snowmobile route, a topographic map and compass are musts for the bushwhack to Spectacle Lake. (See below for other trails to Spectacle.)

The trail begins opposite the parking turnout on NY 10 located on the R (E) just after the second bridge over the West Branch of the Sacandaga River. The trail is marked with a yellow and brown DEC sign.

Immediately upon entering the woods, the hiker passes an iron DEC barrier and begins to climb moderately through mixed hardwoods. This marked snowmobile trail is wide, well-traveled, and pleasant walking. The general direction is WNW. The trail jogs L at 0.2 mi., then quickly R, leveling off a bit at 0.3 mi. It continues through an open hardwood forest following the contour of a ridge. Its width is evidence that it is an old road that was used in more recent years for logging, but the many foundations of buildings around several lakes in this area indicate a long, if lost, history of human use.

An enormous dead tree trunk lies along the trail on the R at 0.4 mi. The trail now begins to descend through a boggy area at 0.5 mi. It continues past this and up a moderate incline to reach a trail junction and DEC register at 0.5 mi.

Marked Trail Entrance

From the junction, a brown and yellow DEC trail sign points R for Dry and Dexter lakes. Take this R. The trail immediately curves L and is smooth and dry, passing through well-spaced mature birch, ash, maple and beech, among other hardwoods. The general direction is due W, continuing over some blowdown and then up a slight rise. At 0.7 mi. the trail makes a gentle curve R and then a slight descent. It is now going in a WNW direction. This is a very attractive section of the old road, wide and softly cushioned by layers of leaves underfoot, with very few rocks.

At 0.8 mi. a sturdy wooden plank bridge crosses a tiny stream. At 1.0 mi. the walking is still through level terrain, easy and pleasant. A brief descent begins at 1.1 mi. and the path continues through an overgrown section, although it is still discernible. At 1.2 mi. the trail descends to an extensive, wildly overgrown wet area and turns R to avoid some of the muckiest areas. There is approximately one-tenth mile of this lush wetland. The heavy shrubbery along both sides provides little or no easy way to traverse this area, indicating that perhaps this wet section is either newly created or temporary.

At 1.3 mi. yet another wet section is encountered. This one, however, is rocky rather than mucky as the water runs downhill, creating a small stream in the trail. The woods, open and lovely, consist of large maple, birch and beech, with scattered boulders adding interest. The trail crosses a stream at 1.4 mi. and the hiker must balance on a slippery, old log bridge. After a brief ascent a bend R occurs, as the trail follows a small stream.

Leaving the stream, the trail climbs a gentle ridge and enters a rocky ravine. The general direction is still due W. At 1.5 mi. a large hemlock obstructs the trail, which is now descending. A heavy growth of witch hobble makes it difficult to go around this obstacle. Now crossing a level section, the trail begins a gentle upward grade and at 1.6 mi. cuts across another wet area, then bends R and exits the ravine.

The old road now goes across the top of the ridge, and at 1.7 mi. there is another muddy, sloppy area, after which the path jogs R and down a tiny incline. At 1.8 mi. the trail bends L to hug the contours of the ridge and descends briefly at 1.9 mi. After it enters a hemlock grove at 2.0 mi. it bends R, and Dry Lake comes into view at 2.1 mi. This is a tiny, attractive lake with rocky shores, cradled in dark green hemlocks.

The trail traverses the N side of the lake and then moves away from the shore and crosses an inlet brook, bending R and going up a draw and over a steep, rocky rib of land that juts into the lake. At 2.3 mi. it descends into a smooth grassy area near the shore of the lake. Here the path is very difficult to follow in midsummer due to abundantly overgrown vegetation. Follow the shore and pick up the trail again in about 50 yds.

Leaving Dry Lake and heading generally W, at 2.4 mi. the trail bends slightly R and at 2.6 mi. jogs L. It enters a ravine shaded by hardwoods mixed with hemlocks. At 2.7 mi. the trail begins to descend through an extremely rocky ravine which is quite steep.

After a considerable drop of nearly 100 ft. from the top of the ridge, the trail reaches the shore of Dexter Lake at 2.9 mi. The trail turns L and crosses the inlet by traversing an old beaver dam and then a large grassy wet area, heading WSW along the shore of Dexter Lake. Snowmobile markers are tacked to trees on the far side of the wet area, although the area itself is without evidence of the trail. There is much evidence of deer browsing. In midsummer and fall, ostrich ferns grow four and five ft. tall.

At 3.0 mi. there is a great quantity of beaver-cut trees and shrubs, leaving large sections of cleared shoreline. For the most part the shoreline is dry, with a preponderance of hemlocks. A dip occurs at 3.1 mi. through a wet area, and the trail continues past a camping area with two or three huge boulders jutting into the water. The water appears to be deep enough for swimming, but it is cluttered with downed tree trunks just below the surface. The S end of the lake is reached at 3.6 mi.

The marked snowmobile trail continues across the end of the lake. The hiker who wishes to explore further should seek the trail to the L, which is so overgrown and unused that a continuation to Spectacle Lake must be considered a bushwhack. The hiker who decides to continue should proceed in a SW direction through a wooded area and, with luck, locate an old logging road, also much overgrown. All paths are barely discernible. Bear WSW from the S end of Dexter Lake. Spectacle Lake will be encountered in approximately 1.0 mi.

Beaver have raised the level of Spectacle Lake at least 3 ft. in recent years. Notice at the W end the concrete foundations and other evidence of the buildings that once graced its shores. Much of the section marked as swamp on the topographic map is currently underwater, thanks to the engineering powers of the beaver. There is no easy way to round the lake to pick up one of the trails back to NY 10 or NY 29. The trails are overgrown, the shores are flooded, and the criss-cross sections of snowmobile trails are often lost to hikers as the trails traverse the swamps. There is only sporadic evidence of an old road, and it is impossible to follow it for any length of time, so the hiker must repeatedly return to higher ground to stay out of the swamps. (See below for a description of the trail to Spectacle Lake from NY 10 and NY 29A.)

Distances: To trail junction, 0.5 mi.; to Dry Lake, 2.1 mi.; to Dexter Lake, 2.9 mi.; to Spectacle Lake (approximate) 4.6 mi. (7.5 km.).

Good Luck Lake

GOOD LUCK LAKE

This charming, shallow lake is an easy walk through attractive level terrain. Its tiny sandy beach provides a nice camping area and a suitable site for swimming. The camping area is extremely popular, however, and overused.

For directions from NY 10 to the trail junction for Good Luck Lake, see above. After reaching the trail junction at 0.5 mi., take the L fork. A wet area is crossed almost immediately. The trail is level at 0.6 mi. and at 0.7 mi. begins a downhill into a depression with a wet area at 0.9 mi. The woods are composed of mature hardwoods and are open and lovely.

Good Luck Lake comes into view on the L at 1.0 mi. The trail is easy and pleasant. Although the lake continues to be glimpsed through the trees, the trail remains on the ridge. At 1.1 mi. a small snowmobile bridge spans a wet area, and another bridge crosses a larger stream at 1.2 mi. The trail rises out of a small ravine after first crossing yet another snowmobile bridge. At 1.2 mi. a big board bridge traverses a section of swamp. The trail jogs L after this and continues up a small hill.

At 1.3 mi. another wet area is crossed, and after a short rise a junction is reached. Good Luck Lake is out of sight. Two signs, one on each side of a triangle in the trail, point to Spectacle Lake to the W.

To reach the shores of Good Luck Lake, seek the unmarked path to the L. It goes down the side of the ridge to the lake and then along the shore for about 0.4 mi. (or 1.8 mi. from the trailhead). There is a large, well-used campsite with a lovely sandy beach along the S shore of Good Luck Lake. Enormous old white pines shade the area.

Additional camping areas along the shore are favorites of canoeists and small boaters (see introduction), but these are difficult for the hiker to reach, thanks to the swamps that comprise the bulk of the shoreline. The E and W ends of Good Luck Lake are exclusively swamplands.

Distances: To first trail junction from NY 10, 0.5 mi.; to Good Luck-Spectacle Lake junction, 1.3 mi.; to Good Luck Lake, 1.8 mi. (2.9 km.).

SPECTACLE LAKE FROM NY 10

Spectacle Lake was probably so named because on a map its shape looks a bit like a pair of old-fashioned spectacles. Years ago there were several buildings on its W end and at least two old roads leading to and around the lake. The lake water level has been raised in recent years by beaver, and the increased swamplands make walking its shore a difficult and wet proposition.

Four snowmobile trails lead to the lake and its vicinity, but these trails are often wet, boggy and difficult to find and follow for the summer hiker. Nevertheless, they provide a challenge and hold promise for adventures in a remote and seldom-visited area. (See above and below for other descriptions of routes to Spectacle Lake.)

To reach a small, attractive campsite on the lakeshore, take the trail from NY 10 to Dry and Dexter lakes (see above). It also leads to Good Luck Lake, Good Luck Mt. Cliffs and the E shore of Spectacle Lake.

At the junction of the cutoff to Good Luck Lake (1.3 mi. from NY 10) go R to reach Spectacle Lake. The trail goes up a little rise and bends R over some very old slippery corduroy at 1.6 mi. The general direction is W heading toward Spectacle Lake. At 1.7 mi., after a few snake-like turns, the trail levels off. Here there are small wet areas to cross before climbing another ridge at 1.8 mi.

The trail continues through a little valley with a stream to the L, and at 2.0 mi. it makes an easy curve R. Up another little hill at 2.1 mi., the trail approaches a large wet area with a trail cutoff R around it. The forest is still open, with mature hardwoods predominant.

Ascending a small hill, the trail enters a ravine. At 2.4 mi. it leaves the ravine and bears R to enter a tiny clearing bordering the shore of Spectacle Lake at 2.6 mi.

Wild pink azalea bushes add color to the little clearing, and although there is limited access to the lake, what one does see is beautiful. It looks as if the trail continues L along the lakeshore, but it goes only to two small clearings in another tenth of a mile and then disappears.

Distances: To first trail junction from NY 10, 0.5 mi.; to Good Luck-Spectacle Lake junction, 1.3 mi.; to Spectacle Lake, 2.6 mi. (4.2 km.).

GOOD LUCK MT. CLIFFS

This short hike ends in a brief but steep ascent to a lovely ledge with wonderful scenery and views. The trailhead is the same used for trips into Good Luck, Dexter, Dry and Spectacle lakes, on NY 10 at the parking turnout just after the second bridge over the West Branch of the Sacandaga River. (See above.)

At the junction of three snowmobile trails at 0.5 mi., take the trail SSW (L) to reach the cutoff for Good Luck Mt. Cliffs and, beyond that, Good Luck Lake. This sign indicates Arietta and Pleasant Lake but it is also the trail to Good Luck Lake and Good Luck Mt. with its cliffs. It does not say Good Luck Lake. Another trail continues slightly R, marked with a sign pointing to Dexter Lake. To the immediate R, and almost hidden in underbrush, a sign says Avery's Place and Piseco. This trail is overgrown and seldom used by hikers since it merely parallels NY 10 for the convenience of snowmobilers.

After taking the SSW turn the trail immediately bends L and passes through a muddy section for about two-tenths of a mile, but the hiker can avoid these mucky sections easily to the L or R. There is a rocky section at 0.8 mi., after which the trail begins a descent. It shares space with a small gurgling stream running down its middle, but a path worn to the L enables one to keep boots dry. Good Luck Lake becomes visible through the trees on the L at 1.0 mi. The trail descends to cross a short plank snowmobile bridge spanning a little brook at 1.3 mi. After traversing a tiny knoll, one encounters a second wooden board bridge at 1.4 mi. Just before crossing this bridge, to the R, one will see a path that is well worn, though unmarked. It immediately begins to climb, following the stream. Take this unmarked footpath, which leads W to Good Luck Mt. and the cliffs.

The path bends R, away from the stream in a WNW direction on a well-defined track that is easy to follow even in midsummer. At 1.5 mi. the stream is encountered again; and this time it can be crossed easily by rock-hopping. Once on the other (W) side the trail proceeds up a draw, clogged here with large, handsome boulders.

The path begins to climb steeply now, beginning the 600-ft. ascent to the top of the cliffs, which can be partially seen in dramatic splendor, at 1.9 mi. on the other side of the draw. Here, next to the path, are several enormous boulders jumbled together to create tiny caves which are most interesting to explore.

Proceeding around the boulders, the path crosses the floor of the gorge, then the stream again at 2.0 mi., and continues up the opposite side, heading due N. A small clearing is crossed at 2.1 mi. where a fork can be discerned. The main footpath goes a bit L, although a jog R will simply take one through a scrubby grove of hemlocks to rejoin the other fork in two-tenths of a mile.

The path climbs rather steeply now, then levels off through the saddle. It bends L at 2.4 mi. to begin a traverse of the ridge. It soon turns R to reach the top of the cliffs at 2.5 mi.

There is a spectacular view of the valley below and hills to the W. On a clear day one can see part of Spectacle Lake to the SW. There are boulders to rest on and the entire ledge is large and shaded by beautiful, twisted white pines—a goal well worth the effort expended.

Distances: To junction, 0.5 mi.; to cutoff and herd path, 1.4 mi.; to top of cliffs, 2.5 mi. (1.6 km.).

SPECTACLE LAKE FROM NY 29A VIA THIRD LAKE

This route to Spectacle Lake is a challenge of endurance, trail finding, map reading, bog hopping—and, in summer, bug swatting. The trail sign off NY 29A says: Spectacle Lake, 6.0; Dexter Lake, 6.5. Do not attempt to reach Dexter Lake by hiking. Consider carefully your desire to reach Spectacle Lake via this snowmobile route.

Access to the trailhead is off NY 29A, 3.0 mi. from the split of NY 29A and NY 10 in the hamlet of Pine Lake. Parking is provided on the S side of the highway, while the trail begins across the road heading N.

The trail begins a moderate downhill until at 0.2 mi., after crossing a wet area, it begins a gradual climb. The forest is mixed with hardwoods and conifers and is fairly smooth under foot. A stream spanned by a wood bridge is crossed at 0.3 mi., and a second smaller one with a washed-out bridge is rock-hopped at 0.4 mi. At 0.6 mi. a large grassy clearing indicates that this is an old beaver pond going back to meadow.

Soon the trail commences to climb up a small rocky ridge curving R. The forest here is very young, as the trees are saplings. A major wet section, created by a small stream filled with black moss, occurs at 0.8 mi.

At 0.9 mi. a junction is reached. A sign pointing L says: "Lakes"; continue L toward "Lakes." Immediately after the junction, the trail bends L. Witch hobble and other shrubs grow in profusion, but the trail is still wide and easy to walk.

A swamp, Burnt Vly, becomes visible on the L at 1.0 mi. At 1.1 the trail begins to climb briefly away from the vly, but skirts its E side for at least the next mile. At 1.2 mi. the trail bends away from Burnt Vly and at 1.3 mi. crosses another section of swamp on a log bridge.

At 1.4 mi., to the L is more swampy area, which is still part of Burnt Vly. After a bend L the trail enters a cathedral of hemlocks. Here the trail is wide and dry. Heading N, it begins climbing a ridge, and at 1.5 mi., now on top of the ridge, enters young hardwoods again. Descending at 1.6 mi., it makes a slight jog to the L. A large stream at 1.7 mi. is crossed on a snowmobile bridge.

An impressive beaver dam is on the R at 1.8 mi. The trail turns away from the beaver dam through a washed-out rocky area, then jogs R and continues due N. Another wet area at 2.1 mi. can be skirted L or R .

The next trail junction reached is a T. Signs point R to Arietta and NY 10, giving no mileage. The L fork is a snowmobile trail to Pleasant Lake. Take the R fork. After a brief ascent and more small wet areas, the trail becomes wilder at 2.6 mi. Follow this trail to another junction at 2.9 mi. A sign here says R to the Arietta Hotel and Log Cabin; straight ahead are Spectacle and Dexter lakes.

Third Lake appears on the R at 2.95 mi. The trail circles this lake, which has a large beaver lodge at its S end. There is a camping area on the R. After leaving the camping area more wet areas are passed, and then the trail descends through a pretty, mature hardwood forest into a small clearing. Another trail goes L, but the main one continues straight ahead. A clearing is passed at 3.3 mi. The trail goes through a thicket of attractive hemlocks and yet another mucky area.

Another junction is reached at 3.4 mi., where a snowmobile bridge crosses a larger stream. Here a sign says: NY 29A via Long Lake to the L; and Dexter Lake 3 mi. straight ahead. (Dexter can be reached only after Spectacle is passed, and the trail is presently lost in the swamps to the hiker, although snowmobilers will no doubt find it.)

After leaving the stream the trail goes through a large wet area. At 3.5 mi. it passes through another stand of evergreens and hemlocks. The trail is wide and shows evidence of wheel ruts indicating recent motorized use.

At 3.6 mi., after climbing a small hill, the trail reaches another junction. (A turn to the R would lead to the E shore of Spectacle and eventually to Good Luck Lake, but this trail is currently unused and completely overgrown.) A turn L leads through another boggy section, after which Spectacle Lake comes into view at 4.0 mi. However, for the next 0.8 mi. it is necessary to walk the high ground to the S to avoid the swampy shores. At 4.8 mi. the faint trail finally descends to the edge of the water, where one can see an enormous rock out in the middle of the lake.

Spectacle Lake is an interesting place to visit, but who would want to live there! Boggy and buggy, it is best visited during cooler times of the year. But it does have an isolated charm, a pristine quality maintained by its inaccessiblity.

Distances: To first junction, 0.9 mi.; to beaver dam, 1.8 mi.; to Third Lake, 2.9 mi.; to junction and large stream crossing, 3.4 mi.; to view of Spectacle Lake, 4.0 mi.; to Spectacle Lake shore, 4.8 mi. (7.8 km.).

Vly near East Canada Creek

IRVING POND, BELLOWS LAKE,
AND HOLMES LAKE

The marked snowmobile trail to Irving Pond, Bellows Lake and Holmes Lake is an invigorating loop trip, but hikers will need to place a car at each end of the trail. To reach the W end of the trail, drive 2.5 mi. along the Benson Road, E from NY 10. There is a dirt road to the N (L) and a brown and yellow DEC sign saying: Irving Pond 1.1 mi.; Bellows Lake 3.0 mi.; and Peters Corners 5.1 mi. These distances are short by 2.2 mi. if a side trip to Holmes Lake is included.

Hikers who wish to do a through trek can spot a car at the E end of this loop trail. To reach the E trailhead, drive an additional 2.5 mi. E along Benson Road to the junction at Peters Corners, where there is ample room to park two or three cars along the shoulder of the road.

Park on the shoulder of Benson Road at the W trailhead and begin walking on Shutts Road, a dirt road not marked by a name sign. There are private property signs posted periodically along the L side. At 0.1 mi. the road begins to climb a moderate grade. It reaches the top of the hill at 0.3 mi. and passes a small house and outbuilding on the L. There are two picturesque apple trees close to the road, which continues straight ahead.

Proceed down a small hill and cross a large wet area at 0.4 mi. A second grassy marsh must be crossed at 0.5 mi. A snowmobile bridge at 0.6 mi. crosses a small stream, after which the trail jogs to the L. The land on the L is still posted, although the road may be used. At 0.7 mi. an extensive wet area has been made muddy and difficult by ruts created by ATV users.

The track becomes less of a road, and more like a trail at 0.8 mi. when it becomes narrow, rocky and rough. A downhill section through hardwoods and brushy undergrowth leads to a grassy area at

0.9 mi.; then the trail makes a jog to the R. The direction of travel is now due N. The land is still posted as private property on the L and R, and a mutilated "No Motorized Vehicles" sign is tacked on a tree at 1.1 mi.

The trail now bends R and is very rocky. It begins to climb gently, heading NNE. At the top of the grade, at 1.2 mi., the trail turns a bit to the R. There is continued evidence of frequent illegal use by motorized vehicles. A large wet area occurs at 1.3 mi., and then the trail descends through another rough, rocky section.

A junction is reached at 1.5 mi. Signs point back to Shutts Road and to the snowmobile trail to Wheelerville (L) and Peters Corners, Bellows Lake and Holmes Lake to the R. Directly ahead is Irving Pond. The trail goes R along the shore of the lake, crossing a small stream at 2.0 mi. It continues circling the lake, crossing a larger inlet at 2.4 mi., which it follows to the top of a small ridge.

At 2.6 mi. a very wet area must be negotiated. The general direction is now N. At 3.0 mi. Bellows Lake comes into view; at 3.1 mi. its shore is reached. Bellows is an attractive, shallow body of water with a shoreline consisting for the most part of marshlands.

The general direction is now ESE as the trail proceeds past Bellows Lake and narrows to a foot path. At 3.5 mi. another small stream and adjacent wet area is crossed. This section passes through an open, lovely forest of mixed hardwoods and conifers. Another small inlet at 3.6 mi. flows into the lake, which can still be glimpsed through the trees. The trail turns away from the lake at 3.8 mi. and goes R, traveling E.

A broken snowmobile bridge is reached at 4.0 mi. At 4.1 mi. the trail passes through an open section of woods and then continues, beginning to climb a ridge and making a bend R. The climbing becomes steeper and is sustained until the crest at 4.4 mi. Traversing the top of the ridge, the trail crosses a large pocket of muck at 4.7 mi.

At 4.8 mi., heading due E, the trail begins to parallel a stream, and a moderate climb uphill begins again. The top of this hillock is reached at 5.0 mi. A leveling occurs at 5.2 mi., and at 5.3 mi. the trail begins to descend. This moderate downhill leads through rocky and wet areas until at 6.2 mi. another trail junction is reached.

The trail L (N) is the route to Holmes Lake, which if taken will add 1.4 mi. to the trip. It is well-used and easy to follow. On the Holmes Lake spur, at 0.3 mi. another wet area occurs, and then an uphill section begins. A small stream runs across the trail at 0.4 mi. and then flows down it for a short way. At 0.5 mi. the trail enters a large, open grassy area and, after passing through this, reaches Holmes Lake at 0.7 mi. A small camping spot is on the shore. Holmes Lake is clear, blue, and very attractive, often visited by fishermen.

From 6.2 mi. (round trip to Holmes Lake is not added), at the junction, the main trail continues S to Peters Corners. Mostly level and traveling through attractive woods, it now descends gently. At 6.3 mi. notice the remains of a building with three pillars of concrete at its entrance.

The trail is very wide and becomes a road again after crossing a stream at 6.4 mi. At 6.6 mi. a big beaver pond is seen on the L. The beaver dam can be seen clearly at the S end of the pond. An abandoned, deteriorating cabin is on the L at 6.7 mi. At 6.8 mi. the trail crosses a wet area, and passes another decaying house at 6.9 mi. The road shows evidence of use by motorized vehicles but is not in good condition. At 7.0 mi. the trail ends. Bear R and pass two homes to exit on the highway at 7.1 mi.

Distances: To Irving Pond, 1.4 mi.; to Bellows Lake, 3.1 mi.; to Holmes Lake spur junction, 6.2 mi. (side trip to Holmes Lake, add 1.7 mi.); to Peters Corners; 7.1 mi. (11.4 km.).

West Lake Access

APPENDIX I

GLOSSARY OF TERMS

Bivouac Camping in the open with improvised shelter or none at all.

Blowdown Tangles of trees that have fallen across the forest floor, often obscuring the trail.

Bushwhacking To make one's way through bushes or undergrowth without the aid of a formal trail.

Col A pass between two peaks or ridgelines.

Corduroy Logs laid side by side across a trail to assist travel in wet areas.

Jeep Trail A woods road still used by four-wheel drive and all-terrain vehicles (ATVs).

Lean-to A three-sided log shelter with an overhanging roof on the open side.

Logging Road A road used to haul logs after lumbering; often found in marshy areas that would be frozen in winter.

Vlei (vly) A low, marshy open area.

APPENDIX II

LEAN-TOS IN THE SOUTHERN REGION

The following is a listing of all lean-tos within the area covered by this guidebook. They are listed according to the guidebook sections, with information on USGS map and location. Unlisted sections have no lean-tos.

Shelter	USGS Map	Location
BENSON, WELLS AND SILVER LAKE WILDERNESS SECTION		
Murphy Lake	Harrisburg	S end of the lake, 4.5 mi. from Pumpkin Hollow Rd.
Chase Lake	Jackson Summit and Caroga Lake	SW shore at end of trails, 2.5 mi. from Pinnacle Rd.
Hamilton Lake Stream	Lake Pleasant	3.4 mi. S of trailhead in Piseco, just past Priests Vly, 50 ft. off trail to E.
Mud Lake	Lake Pleasant	3.0 mi. S of Whitehouse, N shore of Mud Lake.

| Silver Lake | Lake Pleasant | 9.0 mi. S of Whitehouse, E shore of Silver Lake. |

WILCOX LAKE WILD FOREST AND BALDWIN SPRINGS SECTION

| Wilcox Lake | Harrisburg | S shore 150 yds. W of trail end. |
| Wilcox Lake | Harrisburg | SW shore 0.5 mi. E of trail end. |

APPENDIX III

STATE CAMPGROUNDS IN THE SOUTHERN REGION

Public campgrounds have been established by the DEC at many attractive spots throughout the state. Listed below are those campgrounds which might be useful as bases of operations for hiking in the southern Adirondacks region. A complete listing of all campgrounds is contained in a brochure of the New York State Forest Preserve Public Campgrounds entitled "Camping in the Adirondacks." This brochure is available from the DEC, 50 Wolf Rd., Albany, NY 12233.

Caroga Lake Campground. NY 29A, 9 mi. N of Gloversville.
Little Sand Point Campground. Off NY 8, 3 mi. W of Piseco.
Moffitt Beach Campground. NY 8, 4 mi. W of Speculator.
Northampton Beach Campground. NY 30, 1.5 mi. S of Northville.
Point Comfort Campground. Off NY 8, 4 mi. W of Piseco.
Poplar Point Campground. Off NY 8, 2 mi. W of Piseco.
Sacandaga Campground. NY 30, 4 mi. S of Wells.

INDEX

170

172

Join a Chapter

Three-quarters of ADK members belong to the chapter in their area. Those not wishing to join a particular chapter join ADK as members-at-large.

Local chapter membership brings you an easy way to join in on the fun of outings and social activities or the reward of working on trails, conservation, and education projects at the local level. And you can still participate in all regular Club activities and receive all the regular benefits.

Adirondak Loj ...... North Elba
Albany
Algonquin ...... Plattsburgh
Black River ...... Watertown
Cold River ...... Long Lake
Finger Lakes ...... Ithaca-Elmira
Genesee Valley ...... Rochester
Glens Falls
Hurricane Mountain ...... Keene
Iroquois ...... Utica
Keene Valley
Knickerbocker ...... New York City & Vicinity
Lake Placid
Laurentian ...... Canton-Potsdam
Long Island
Mid-Hudson ...... Poughkeepsie
Mohican ...... Westchester & Putnam Co., N.Y. / Fairfield Co., CT
New York ...... Metropolitan Area *
Niagara Frontier ...... Buffalo
North Jersey ...... Bergen County, NJ
North Woods ...... Saranac Lake-Tupper Lake
Onondaga ...... Syracuse
Penn's Woods ...... Harrisburg, PA
Ramapo ...... Rockland Co.
Schenectady
Shatagee Woods ...... Malone
Susquehanna ...... Oneonta

*   Special Requirements Apply

Membership

To Join

Send this form with payment to **Adirondack Mountain Club • 174 Glen Street • Glens Falls • N.Y. 12801**, or drop it off at the Adirondak Loj.

Name _____

Address _____

City _____ State _____ Zip _____

Home Telephone ( )

☐ I want to join as a member-at-large.

☐ I want to join as a _____ Chapter member.

List family members & children under 18 to be enrolled:

Spouse _____ Birthdate _____

Child _____

Child _____

Child _____

Bill my: ☐ VISA ☐ MASTERCARD Acct. # _____

Exp. Date _____

☐ I have read and accepted the ADK pledge _____
signature (required for charge)

ADK is a non-profit, tax-exempt organization. Membership fees are tax deductible, as allowed by law. Please allow 6-8 weeks for receipt of first issue of **Adirondac.**

Check Membership Level:

☐ Life $750*

☐ Forest Preserve $200*

☐ Patron $100*

☐ Supporting . . . . $ 60*

☐ Contributing . . . . . . $ 40*

☐ Family . . . . $ 35*

☐ Adult . . . . $ 30

☐ Senior Family . . . . . $ 25*

☐ Senior (65+) . . . . . . $ 20

☐ Junior (under 18) . . $ 15

☐ Student
(18+, full time) . . $ 15

School _____

*Includes associate/family members

Membership Rewards

- **Discovery:**
  ADK can broaden your horizons by introducing you to new places, recreational activities, and interests.

- **Enjoyment:**
  Being outdoors more and loving it more.

- **People:**
  Meeting others and sharing the fun.

- **Adirondac Magazine:**
  Ten times a year.

- **Member Discounts:**
  20% off on publications, 10% on lodge stays, and reduced rates for educational programs.

- **Satisfaction:**
  Knowing you're doing your part and that future generations will enjoy the wilderness as you do.

Adirondack **ADK** Mountain Club

CONSERVATION
RECREATION
EDUCATION